FAMILY HOUSES
MAISONS UNIFAMILIALES
EINFAMILIENHÄUSER

FAMILY HOUSES
MAISONS UNIFAMILIALES
EINFAMILIENHÄUSER

EVERGREEN

EVERGREEN is an imprint of

Taschen GmbH

© 2005 TASCHEN GmbH

Hohenzollernring 53, D-50672 Köln

www.taschen.com

Editor Editrice Redakteur:
Simone Schleifer

Editorial assistance Assistante d'édition Verlagsassistentin:
Marta Serrats

English translation Traduction anglaise Englische Übersetzung:
Matthew Connell

French translation Traduction française Französische Übersetzung:
Marion Westerhoff

German translation Traduction allemande Deutsche Übersetzung:
Susanne Engler

Proof reading Relecture Korrektur lesen:
Matthew Clarke, Marie-Pierre Santamarina

Art director Direction artistique Art Direktor:
Mireia Casanovas Soley

Graphic design and layout Mise en page et maquette Graphische Gestaltung und Layout:
Diego González

Printed by Imprimé en Gedruckt durch:
Artes Gráficas Toledo

ISBN: 3-8228-4190-0

Contents Index Inhalt

010-019   **House in Miravalle**   Maison à Miravalle   Haus in Miravalle

020-027   **X House**   Maison X   X Haus

028-033   **Berman House**   Maison Berman   Haus Berman

034-039   **Rooftecture M**

040-047   **De Blas House**   Maison De Blas   Haus De Blas

048-055   **CH House**   Maison CH   CH Haus

056-063   **Schmitz House**   Maison Schmitz   Haus Schmitz

064-071   **Crescent House**   Maison Crescent   Crescent Haus

072-077   **Furniture-House**   Maison-meuble   Möbel-Haus

078-085   **Mediterranean Dwelling**   Habitation méditerranéenne   Mediterranes Wohnhaus

086-093   **House on Iritahama Beach**   Habitation sur la plage de Iritahama   Haus am Strand von Iritahama

094-101   **Eremo Residence**   Résidence Eremo   Haus Eremo

102-111   **Residence in Pacific Palisades**   Résidence à Pacific Palisades   Haus in Pacific Palisades

112-119   **Chalet in Lissago**   Pavillon à Lissago   Chalet in Lissago

120-125   **Tennessee River Residence**   Résidence Tennessee River   Haus Tennessee River

126-133   **Bassil Residence**   Résidence Bassil   Haus Bassil

134-141   **Cutipol House**   Maison Cutipol   Cutipol Haus

142-149   **Aiguablava**

150-155   **Cromer Residence**   Résidence Cromer   Haus Cromer

156-163   **House on Cascade Lake**   Maison à côté du lac Cascade   Haus am See Cascade

164-169   **Wilson Residence**   Résidence Wilson   Wilson Haus

170-175   **House and Art Gallery**   Habitation et galerie d'art   Haus und Kunstgalerie

176-183   **Turba House**   Maison Turba   Haus Turba

184-189   **Spring Prairie Residence**   Résidence Spring Prairie   Haus Spring Prairie

190-195   **Coppola Residence**   Résidence Coppola   Haus Coppola

196-201   **Sutterlüty House**   Maison Sutterlüty   Haus Sutterlüty

202-209   **Adda Valley Residence**   Résidence Adda Valley   Haus Adda Valley

210-215   **Villa Novellino**

216-223   **House in Concepcion**   Maison à Concepcion   Haus in Concepcion

224-231   **Villa 1**

232-241   **Spine Residence**   Résidence Spine   Haus Spine

242-247   **Clement Residence**   Résidence Clement   Clement Residenz

248-255   **C House**   Maison C   Haus C

256-263   **Smarthouse**

264-273   **Lingg Residence**   Résidence Lingg   Haus Lingg

274-283   **Las Encinas Residence**   Résidence Las Encinas   Residenz Las Encinas

284-289   **Residence in Hyogo**   Résidence à Hyogo   Haus in Hyogo

290-295   **Double L**   Deux L   Doppeltes L

296-301   **Cliff Residence**   Résidence Cliff   Residenz Cliff

302-309   **Tea Gardens Residence**   Résidence Tea Gardens   Tea Gardens Haus

310-315   **House in High Bridge**   Habitation à High Bridge   Haus in High Bridge

316-323   **House on Mount Fuji**   Habitation sur le mont Fuji   Haus am Fuß des Berges Fuji

324-329   **YG House**   Maison YG   Haus YG

330-335   **Howard House**   Maison Howard   Haus Howard

336-341   **Into House**   Maison Into   Haus Into

342-349   **Rosenthal House**   Maison Rosenthal   Haus Rosenthal

350-357   **Y House**   Maison Y   Haus Y

358-365   **Villa Man-bow**

366-371   **Tree House**   Maison Arbre   Baumhaus

372-381   **Rose Residence**   Résidence Rose   Rose Residenz

382-383   **Photo Credits**   Crédits photographiques   Fotonachweis

The family house represents a paradigm in the evolution of architecture, as it has been a privileged realm in which architects have been able to freely experiment-hence, they have used it as a tool to propose different lifestyles and to speculate on the changes that new social habits will mean for families. The technological innovations filtering ever more quickly into our homes offer a glimpse of what the house of the future will be like: many experts foresee a scenario in which the traditional distribution of space will be replaced by integrated spaces and functional solutions that redefine the concept of the home and satisfy the diverging needs of all the members of a family.

Family Houses presents several examples of this emerging residential architecture, linked by the manner in which architects propose innovative and experimental solutions. Refinement in the finishing, restraint in the layout and painstaking integration of construction elements into the surroundings are just some of the criteria that have to be taken into account in their designs. Although each of the houses featured in this selection follows its own path stylistically, they all surprise us with their technical resources and the range of sensations they induce.

Although none of these houses could be described as extravagant, they are all implicitly exclusive, as each stems from a very personal commission; individual clients' preferences and budgets will always determine unique projects. Their architects were given a unique opportunity to expand their creativity: in meeting their clients' needs, they were able to contribute new design ideas or test functional solutions and building methods. In the end, the designers of such houses are responsible for stimulating our senses, broadening our perspectives and creating spaces that focus our attention on what is essential in life. In all of these houses, the architects have paid special attention to the dynamics found when different family members live together, and they have thus geared their efforts toward finding a balance between design for design's sake and functionality.

The other fundamental characteristic linking the homes in *Family Houses* is the dialogue they all establish with their surroundings: the formal expression of each and every house reveals an intimate understanding of the unique qualities of the landscape that surrounds it. This concept has served as the starting point for innovative designs that distil a special synergy between house and site. The book you have before you illustrates not just the transformation of the concept of the family house, but also the sophisticated and meticulous experimentation that is required to produce unique homes adjusted to the needs of each family.

Dans le cadre de l'évolution architecturale, la maison unifamiliale est une typologie paradigmatique. En effet, c'est un champ d'expérimentation que les architectes ont utilisé pour créer des styles de vie différents et pour méditer sur les changements engendrés par les nouvelles habitudes sociales sur le milieu familial. Les avancées technologiques parviennent de plus en plus vite dans nos foyers, nous permettant d'imaginer la maison de demain : un scénario prônant l'abandon de la distribution spatiale traditionnelle, au profit d'espaces intégrés et de solutions fonctionnelles qui nous rapprochent d'une nouvelle conception de l'habitat satisfaisant les besoins de chaque membre de la famille.

Maisons unifamiliales est un recueil d'exemples de cette architecture résidentielle émergente, d'habitations dont le dénominateur commun est la création de solutions innovatrices et expérimentales. Le choix épuré des finitions, la distribution harmonieuse des espaces de vie ou le soin apporté pour intégrer l'espace à l'environnement, définissent certains des concepts de base de ces projets. Même si les résidences présentées suivent des voies différentes, toutes surprennent par la qualité de construction et par le kaléidoscope d'impressions qu'elles offrent.

Dépourvue d'extravagance, l'exclusivité est implicite dans tous ces projets, reflets d'une commande très personnalisée. Car à chaque client correspond, au gré de ses désirs et volontés, un projet unique. De son côté, l'architecte peut donner libre cours à son activité créatrice, apporter de nouvelles idées et essayer des solutions novatrices sur les plans fonctionnel et architectural. Ceux qui conçoivent nos maisons s'engagent à stimuler nos sens, à élargir nos perspectives et à créer des espaces qui nous mènent à l'essentiel de la vie. Dans chacun de ces projets, les architectes ont été particulièrement attentifs à la cohabitation entre tous les membres de la famille, s'efforçant d'instaurer l'équilibre délicat entre construction et habitabilité.

Maisons unifamiliales traite d'un autre thème essentiel qui est le dialogue avec le paysage : tous les projets laissent transparaître l'harmonie entre l'expression formelle et la singularité de l'environnement où ils sont implantés, un accord servant de point de départ à des solutions innovantes qui essaient de s'intégrer au paysage pour parvenir à une synergie d'ensemble. Cet ouvrage est une collection unique d'exemples montrant à la fois l'évolution du concept d'habitation unifamiliale et l'expérimentation architecturale, sur la base d'épures d'une très grande précision, visant à créer des maisons presque sur mesures, adaptées aux besoins de chaque famille.

Das Einfamilienhaus hat, was die architektonische Entwicklung betrifft, Modellcharakter. Dieser Gebäudetyp ermöglicht es den Architekten, unter hervorragenden Bedingungen zu experimentieren. Sie haben es als ein Mittel genutzt, um andere Lebensstile aufzugreifen und über die Veränderungen nachzudenken, die neue soziale Gewohnheiten im traditionellen Familienmodell verursachen. Die technologischen Innovationen erreichen unser Zuhause immer schneller und nehmen vorweg, wie das Haus der Zukunft sein wird: eine Wohnumgebung, für die Viele vorhersagen, dass die traditionelle Raumaufteilung zugunsten von integrierten Räumen und funktionellen Lösungen aufgegeben wird un somit ein neues Raumkonzept entstht, dass die verschiedenen Bedürfnisse aller Familienmitglieder erfüllent.

In *Einfamilienhäuser* wird eine interessante Zusammenstellung dieser neuen Wohnhausarchitektur vorgestellt, deren Gemeinsamkeit die Suche nach innovativen und experimentellen Lösungen ist. Eine sorgfältige Auswahl der Oberflächenmaterialien, die maßvolle Verteilung der Fläche und die gewissenhafte Suche nach Räumen, die sich in die Umgebung integrieren, sind einige der Kennzeichen dieser Architektur. Obwohl jedes der vorgestellten Häuser anders ist, überraschen uns alle aufgrund der hohen baulichen Qualität und der Vielzahl von Eindrücken, die sie hervorrufen.

Diese Häuser sind nicht extravagant, aber exklusiv und einzigartig, da jedes davon durch die persönlichen Wünsche und das zur Verfügung stehende Budget des jeweiligen Kunden geprägt ist. Der Architekt hat bei dieser Art von Bauvorhaben die Möglichkeit, seine kreative Arbeit zu vertiefen, neue Ideen anzubringen und innovative funktionelle und bauliche Lösungen einzusetzen. Diejenigen, die unsere Häuser entwerfen, sind dafür verantwortlich, unsere Sinne anzuregen, unsere Perspektive zu erweitern und Räume zu schaffen, die uns dem Wesentlichen im Leben näher bringen. In all diesen Häusern haben die Architekten besondere Aufmerksamkeit auf das Zusammenleben aller Familienmitglieder gerichtet und sich auf ein Gleichgewicht zwischen dem physischen Gebäude und der Bewohnbarkeit konzentriert.

Ein weiterer, grundlegender Aspekt der Projekte, die in *Einfamilienhäuser* vorgestellt werden, ist der Dialog mit der Landschaft. Bei all diesen Häusern existiert eine Kommunikation zwischen dem formalen Ausdruck der Architektur und der Einzigartigkeit der Umgebung, in der sie sich befinden, ein Gleichgewicht, das den Ausgangspunkt für innovative Lösungen bildet, die mit der Landschaft experimentieren, um ein Zusammenwirken aller Elemente zu bewirken. Dieses Buch ist somit ein einzigartiger Beweis dafür, dass ein Umdenken im Konzept des Einfamilienhauses stattfindet und dass mit klaren Schemata und einer sorgfältigen Ausführung experimentiert wird, durch die Wohnhäuser fast nach Maß entstehen, die sich an die Bedürfnisse jeder Familie anpassen.

House in Miravalle
Maison à Miravalle
Haus in Miravalle

Miravalle, Ecuador

The biggest challenge here was to take full advantage of this house's surroundings and at the same time preserve the privacy of its occupants. Thus, the architects designed a floor plan in the shape of a boomerang whose interior face is lined with glass walls; this conceit provides a panoramic view from any part of the house. In the main wing, a terrace that starts in the dining room extends as though it were rising to Cotopaxi mount. The opposite wing culminates in the pool, beside which an elevated walkway gives views out onto the valley at its feet. The glass used in the façade was treated so that it would have a greenish hue, helping it to blend into its surroundings; when seen from the opposite side of the valley, the house is camouflaged by the landscape.

Le plus grand défi de ce projet consistait à réaliser une habitation tirant parti au maximum des avantages de l'environnement qui l'entoure tout en préservant l'intimité de ses occupants. Face à ces exigences, les architectes ont choisi de concevoir un plan en forme de boomerang dont les murs de l'angle intérieur sont entièrement vitrés. Cette option offre une immense vue panoramique où que l'on soit dans la maison. Dans l'aile principale, une terrasse, partant de la salle à manger, s'étire comme si elle voulait atteindre le mont Cotopaxi. L'aile opposée est parachevée par une piscine, d'où part une passerelle latérale s'élevant à l'instar d'un mirador au-dessus de la vallée qui s'étend à ses pieds. La surface vitrée de la façade est en verre traité de couleur verdâtre, facilitant son intégration à l'environnement : de l'autre côté de la vallée, la construction se fond ainsi au paysage.

Die größte Herausforderung bei dieser Planung lag darin, die Vorteile der Umgebung so weit wie möglich zu nutzen und gleichzeitig die Privatsphäre der Bewohner zu bewahren. Unter diesen Gesichtspunkten entwarfen die Architekten einen Grundriss mit der Form eines Bumerangs. Im Hauptflügel erstreckt sich eine Terrasse, die am Esszimmer beginnt, so weit, dass sie den Eindruck erweckt, den Berg Cotopaxi berühren zu wollen. Der entgegengesetzte Flügel hat am Ende einen Swimmingpool, umgeben von einer erhöhten Plattform, die zu einem Aussichtspunkt über das Tal wird, das ihr zu Füßen liegt. Das Fensterglas in der Fassade wurde in einer grünlichen Farbe getönt. So passt sich das Gebäude besser in die Umgebung ein und ist von der anderen Seite des Tales aus in der Landschaft nur schwer zu entdecken.

The glass façade allows the inhabitants to enjoy the landscape and also enables natural light to flood into the interior.

La structure de verre de la façade permet à la fois de jouir du paysage et de baigner l'intérieur de lumière naturelle.

Die verglaste Struktur der Fassade lässt den Blick auf die Landschaft frei und sokann reichlich Licht ins Innere strömen.

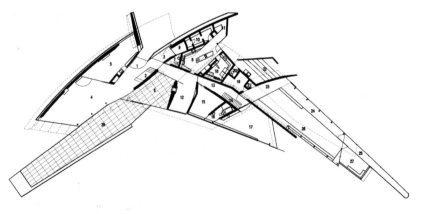

› Ground floor Rez-de-chaussée Erdgeschoss

› First floor Premier étage Erstes Obergeschoss

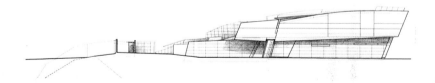

› Elevations Élévations Aufrisse

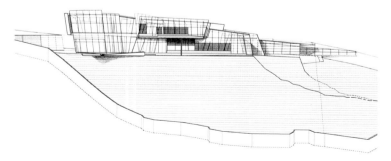

› Section Section Schnitt

The high ceilings and the distinctive sloping façade give a sense of openness and create a dynamic indoor space.

La hauteur importante de la toiture et l'angle d'inclinaison inhabituel de la façade produisent une sensation d'espace et dynamisent l'univers intérieur.

Die Decken sind sehr hoch und die Fassade hat eine ungewöhnliche Neigung, was die Räume sehr weit und dynamisch wirken lässt.

X House
Maison X
X Haus

Cañete, Peru

This house forms part of a complex of two residences separated by a terraced area, nestled in an uneven, desert site. As the architects felt the structure of the X House should take up most of the site, it was designed as a solid volume that would be anchored into the ground. They designed a two-story program: while one story is used as bedrooms, the other is taken up by the kitchen, dining room and salon/terrace. The floor on the upper level comprises a wooden deck that extends to the edge of a narrow, elongated pool, which stretches across the side of the house facing the sea and hangs over the stairway that connects the two levels. Should bad weather require it, the dining room can be closed off from the terrace by means of a series of detachable panels when they are removed, however, the boundary between interior and exterior disappears.

Cette habitation fait partie d'un complexe de deux résidences séparées par un terrain en terrasse, enclavé dans une zone abrupte au climat désertique. Les architectes ont décidé que la structure de la maison X devait occuper la majeure partie du terrain et être conçue comme un volume massif ancré sur la terre. Le plan comprend deux étages : un réservé aux chambres à coucher et l'autre accueillant les pièces à vivre -cuisine, salle à manger et salon/terrasse-. Le niveau supérieur est revêtu d'un parquet de lames de bois qui s'achève au bord d'une piscine étroite et allongée. Ce bassin s'étire le long de la façade orientée vers la mer et reste suspendu à la hauteur de l'entrée de l'escalier qui relie les deux niveaux. La salle à manger peut se fermer devant la terrasse si les conditions météorologiques l'exigent, grâce à deux panneaux démontables. En leur absence, la frontière entre l'intérieur et l'extérieur est totalement imperceptible.

Dieses Haus gehört zu einem Komplex mit zwei Häusern in einer Wüstenregion, die durch ein terrassenförmig angelegtes Gelände getrennt sind. Die Architekten entschieden, dass die Struktur des Hauses Equis den größten Teil des Grundstücks einnehmen sollte und schufen ein solides, gut in der Erde verankertes Gebäude. Die Wohnbereiche sind über zwei Stockwerke verteilt, in einem liegen die Schlafzimmer und in dem anderen Wohnzimmer, Küche, Speisezimmer und Wohnterrasse. Der Boden des oberen Stockwerks ist mit Holzdielen belegt, die bis zum Rand eines kleinen, länglichen Swimmingpools reichen. Dieser Pool erstreckt sich entlang der ganzen Fassade zum Meer hin bis zu der Höhe der Treppenöffnung, die beide Stockwerke verbindet. Das Speisezimmer kann mithilfe abmontierbarer Platten von der Terrasse getrennt werden, wenn die Wetterbedingungen dies notwendig machen. Wenn diese Platten nicht angebracht sind, sind die Grenzen zwischen Innen und Außen fast nicht definiert.

The striking pool extends along the terrace and even stretches beyond it, over an opening carved by the stairway.

La piscine originale file le long de la terrasse et en dépasse même les limites pour s'étirer au-dessus de l'escalier.

Der einzigartige Swimmingpool verläuft am Rand der Terrasse und überschreitet sogar die Begrenzungen dieser Struktur, um sich bis zur Treppenöffnung hinzuziehen.

Ochre and sandy yellow were the colors chosen for the exterior, recalling Pre-Columbian buildings this conceals the damage caused by sand blowing in from the desert.

Les façades s'affichent dans les tons ocre et sable, identiques à ceux utilisés dans l'architecture précolombienne, pour masquer l'usure provoquée par le sable du désert.

Die Fassaden sind in Ocker- und Sandtönen gestrichen, ähnlich denen der präkolumbischen Bauten. So sieht man kaum, wie stark der Wüstensand die Fassaden angreift.

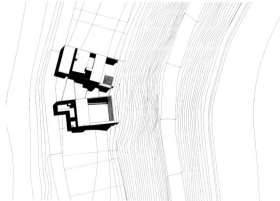

› Situation plan Plan de situation Lageplan

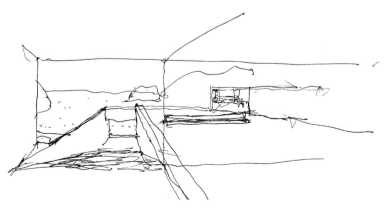

› Sketch Esquisse Skizze

The edge of one side of the upper floor is lined by a stone bench that establishes a close relationship with the surroundings.

Un banc de pierre festonne le bord latéral de l'étage supérieur, établissant un lien étroit avec l'environnement.

Am seitlichen Rand des oberen Stockwerkes verläuft eine Steinbank, die eine enge Beziehung zur Umgebung aufbaut.

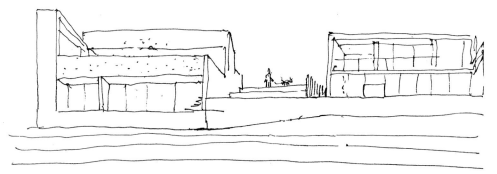

The kitchen occupies a small space on the upper level and is closely linked to the dining room by means of an interior window.

La cuisine, qui occupe une petite surface à l'étage supérieur, est très étroitement reliée à la salle à manger par le biais d'une fenêtre intérieure

Die Küche nimmt eine kleine Fläche im Obergeschoss ein und ist durch ein Fenster im Inneren mit dem Speisezimmer verbunden.

Berman House
Maison Berman
Haus Berman

Joadja, Australia

A steep and rocky outcrop overlooking a canyon is the backdrop to this unusual home. The architectural composition is based on a horizontal scheme organized around a single story with two levels: the lower level, which is fixed to the cliff, contains the day areas, and the upper level, which is closed and intimate, the bedrooms. This disjunction can also be seen from the exterior, as it marks the starting point of the roofs, which extend sinuously over both volumes. Although the main volume of the house was built in concrete, the roof structure is made from curving metal beams of different radii, to achieve an undulating effect. The cantilevered balcony that juts out over the canyon is attacked to the structure by means of diagonal braces that further emphasize its apparent defiance of gravity.

Une zone rocheuse et escarpée enfermée dans le canyon creusé par le fleuve qui le traverse, caractérise l'atmosphère qui entoure cette résidence particulière. La composition architecturale s'intègre dans un schéma horizontal organisé sur un étage à deux niveaux : l'étage inférieur, situé au bord du précipice, comprend les zones de jour, et l'étage supérieur, clôt et intime, contient les chambres. La dénivellation est également perceptible de l'extérieur, car elle marque le point de séparation entre les toitures qui s'étendent en ondulations, couronnant les deux volumes. Les fondations sont en béton, mais la structure des toitures est construite à partir de poutres métalliques incurvées de différents diamètres pour créer l'effet d'ondulation. Le balcon en encorbellement, surplombant la falaise, est amarré à la structure métallique grâce à des bras en diagonale, exaltant encore davantage l'effet d'apesanteur de la composition.

Dieses einzigartige Haus liegt in einer felsigen und schroffen Region an einer Schlucht, durch die ein Fluss verläuft. Die architektonische Gestaltung geht von einem horizontalen Konzept mit zwei Stockwerken aus. Im Untergeschoss, das zur Schlucht hin liegt, befinden sich die Räume für den Tag, während das Obergeschoss geschlossener und intimer ist und die Schlafzimmer aufnimmt. Den Höhenunterschied nimmt man auch von außen wahr, da er den Ausgangspunkt der Dächer markiert, die sich kurvig über beide Gebäudeteile ziehen. Die Mauern sind aus Beton, während die Dächer aus gebogenen Stahlträgern mit unterschiedlichen Radien konstruiert wurden, um die Wellenform zu erreichen. Der Balkon liegt auf einem Vorsprung über der Schlucht und wird an der Metallstruktur durch zwei diagonale Arme gehalten, was die Komposition noch schwereloser wirken lässt.

The spectacular location of this house determined the design for a house that needed to be both emphatic and light.

L'emplacement spectaculaire définit les lignes d'un objet architectural léger et contondant à la fois.

Die wundervolle Umgebung bildete die Grundlage für die Konstruktion, die massig und gleichzeitig leicht wirkt.

The cantilevered balcony was conceived of as an extension of the living room and as a spectacular promotory from which to admire the steep cliffs.

Le balcon en encorbellement se présente comme le prolongement du salon, à l'instar d'un mirador spectaculaire qui capte les profondeurs de l'abîme.

Der Balkon auf einem Vorsprung ist wie eine Verlängerung des Wohnzimmers angelegt. Er dient als ein wundervoller Aussichtspunkt über die Schlucht.

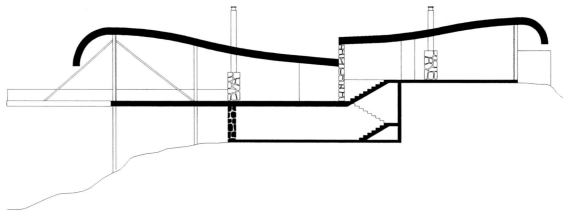

› Longitudinal section   Section longitudinale   Längsschnitt

This suspended walkway has a glass balustrade that allows the inhabitants to freely take in the landscape, as well as increasing the sense of weightlessness.

Cette passerelle suspendue est festonnée d'une balustrade de verre qui libère la vue sur le paysage et accentue l'effet d'apesanteur.

Dieser hängende Laufsteg wird von einem verglastenGeländer gehalten, durch dass man die Landschaft sieht und das Gefühl von Schwerelosigkeit bekommt.

Rooftecture M

Maruoka, Japan

Rooftecture M serves two functions: besides being a residence, the owner also wanted a workshop that would both exude calm and offer panoramic views of the landscape. So, the architect decided to design the first level –the location of the workshop– using a single wall along the western side that wraps around to enclose the room and ends in the eastern façade. To insulate the house from noise pollution, along the east-west axis the structure was fitted with a sheet of steel. The private rooms –the bedrooms, living room and dining room– are located in the zones nestled deepest inside the house, furthest from the gaze of neighbours, in order for family life to carry on as normal. Accodingly, the bedrooms are on the first floor, while the kitchen, dining room, living room and bathroom are on the ground floor. On the other hand, the workshop is on the north side of the house, on the first level, in a glazed area open to the outside.

Rooftecture M a deux fonctions : une habitation à laquelle le propriétaire voulait ajouter un atelier doté d'un espace tranquille et d'une grande perspective visuelle. Pour réaliser ce souhait, l'architecte a conçu le premier niveau sur un seul plan pour accueillir l'atelier : le mur du côté ouest ondule pour clore l'espace et s'achève dans la façade sud. Pour isoler la maison des nuisances sonores extérieures, la structure est revêtue sur l'axe est-ouest d'une plaque d'acier. Les sphères de vie privée –chambres à coucher, salon et salle à manger– sont situées dans les zones les plus profondes, les plus protégées des regards indiscrets, permettant ainsi une vie de famille agréable. Les chambres à coucher sont situées au premier étage; la cuisine, la salle à manger, le salon et la salle de bains, au rez-de-chaussée. Par contre, l'atelier est situé au nord de la maison, au premier étage, dans une zone ouverte sur l'extérieur et recouverte de verre.

Außer einem Wohnhaus wünschte sich der Eigentümer eine Werkstatt, die ruhig und visuell anregend wirkt. Deshalb legte der Architekt die erste Ebene, auf der die Werkstatt liegt, auf einer einzigen Fläche an. Die westliche Seitenmauer ist gewellt und schließt den Raum ab, sie hört an der Ostfassade auf. Um das Haus vom Lärm zu isolieren, wurde die Struktur der Ost-West-Achse mit einer Stahlplatte verkleidet. Die privaten Räume, also Schlafzimmer, Wohnzimmer und Esszimmer, befinden sich in den ninteren Räumen, so dass sie vor Blicken geschützt sind. Hier kann sich die Familie entspannen. Die Schlafzimmer liegen im ersten Stock, die Küche, das Esszimmer, das Wohnzimmer und das Bad im Erdgeschoss. Die Werkstatt liegt im nördlichen Teil des Hauses im ersten Stock in einem Bereich, der nach außen offen und mit Glas verkleidet ist.

The three dominant materials in the house are steel, in the structure; wood, in the interior; and glass, in some of the walls.

Les trois matériaux qui prédominent sont l'acier de la structure, le bois de l'intérieur et le verre de certains murs.

Die drei vorherrschenden Materialien sind der Stahl der Struktur, das Holz im Inneren und das Glas an einigen der Wände.

住いの提案

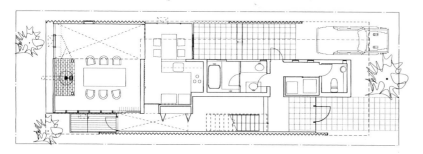

› First floor   Premier étage   Erstes Obergeschoss

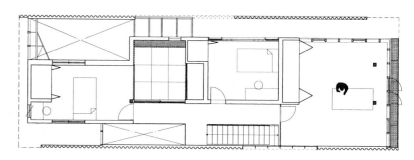

› Second floor   Deuxième étage   Zweites Obergeschoss

De Blas House
Maison De Blas
Haus De Blas

Sevilla la Nueva, Spain

The De Blas House is a brilliant exercise in architecture, consisting of a glass box poised on top of a concrete platform. It is situated on a hill to the southwest of Madrid, and to the north it enjoys spectacular views of the Sierra. Its concrete platform emerges from the ground and creates an air of solidity, while the functional organization of the house is clear and simple: the bedrooms, living room and dining room are placed in the front, facing north; and the services area, bathrooms and circulation are relegated to the back. The rooms display two distinct treatments: to the north, the square windows frame striking panoramic views, and to the south, sunlight filters in through small holes cut into the top of the wall. The glass box above the platform is a kind of watchtower, reached from inside the house.

La maison De Blas est une superbe étude architecturale. L'édifice composé d'une structure de verre posée sur un bloc de béton, est implanté sur le haut d'une colline au sud-ouest de Madrid, et, orienté vers le nord, jouit de splendides vues sur la montagne. Le volume de béton, ancré dans la terre, offre un aspect solide et rond. L'organisation fonctionnelle de ce corps architectural est claire et simple : les chambres à coucher, le salon et la salle à manger sont situés à l'avant de la maison, orientés vers le nord, et la zone de services, salles de bains et couloirs est reléguée à l'arrière. Les pièces à vivre de ce niveau intègrent la nature de deux façons distinctes : au nord, les fenêtres carrées délimitent de belles vues panoramiques, et au sud, la lumière et le ciel s'infiltrent par des petites ouvertures percées dans le haut du mur. Le bloc de verre, posé sur la plate-forme, est un mirador accessible depuis la maison.

Das Haus De Blas ist ein Meisterwerk der Architektur. Das Gebäude, das aus einem verglasten Körper auf einem Betonblock besteht, befindet sich auf einem Hügel im Südwesten von Madrid. In Richtung Norden hat man einen wunderbaren Blick über die benachbarte Gebirgskette. Der Betonkörper wurde im Boden verankert und wirkt fest und massiv. Die funktionelle Aufteilung ist klar und einfach, die Schlafzimmer, das Wohnzimmer und das Esszimmer befinden sich im vorderen Teil des Hauses nach Norden, und die funktionellen Bereiche, Badezimmer und Flure liegen nach hinten. Die Räume in diesem Stockwerk schließen die Natur auf zwei verschiedene Weisen ein, im Norden unterstreichen die quadratischen Fenster den schönen Panoramablick, während nach Süden hin das Licht und der Himmel durch kleine Öffnungen oben in der Wand zu sehen sind. Der Glaskasten auf einer Plattform ist ein verglaster Balkon mit Aussicht, den man vom Wohnhaus aus betritt.

The roof, a white steel expanse crowning, crowns the glass box, is supported up by eight columns.

La couverture, un plan d'acier peint en blanc, coiffe le mirador soutenu par huit colonnes au double profil.

Das Dach aus flachem, weiß gestrichenen Stahl krönt den Aussichtspunkt, der von acht Säulen mit doppeltem Profil gehalten wird.

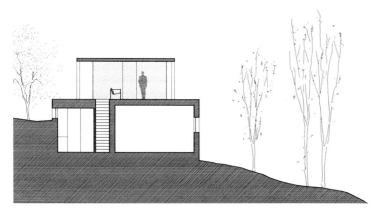

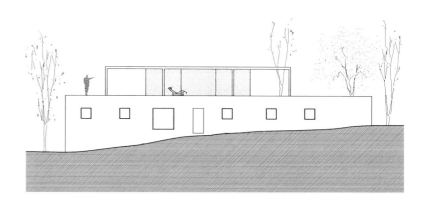

› Sections   Sections   Schnitte

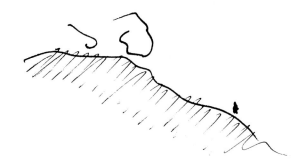

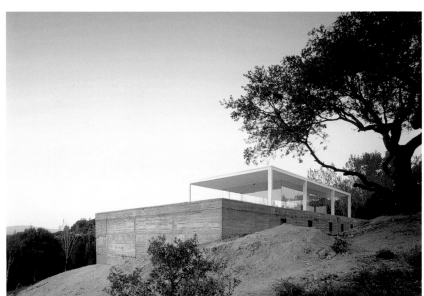

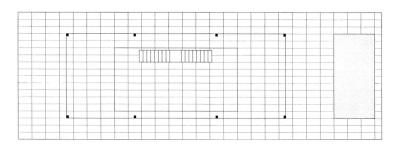

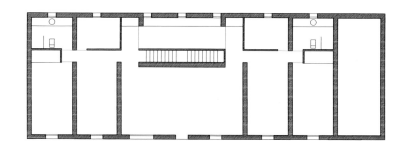

› Plans   Plans   Grundrisse

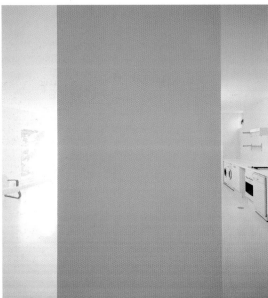

The stairway that connects the box to the rooms acts as a boundary between the kitchen and the living room.

L'escalier qui communique avec les pièces à vivre joue le rôle d'élément séparateur entre la cuisine et le salon.

Die Verbindungstreppe zwischen den Räumen dient als Trennelement zwischen der Küche und dem Wohnzimmer.

The glass shelter offers spectacular views of the surrounding area.

Le container de verre protège le mirador du haut duquel on peut admirer les splendides vues du paysage environnant.

Von dem verglasten Balkon aus hat man einen wunderbaren Ausblick über die umliegende Landschaft.

CH House
Maison CH
CH Haus

Barcelona, Spain

This house, designed as a family home for a couple with three children, adapts to its elongated site by taking the shape of a prism whose smaller faces form the main façades. Most of the openings in the outer casing of the house are set in these façades, and the bedrooms are located behind them. The east façade conceals the children's bedrooms, which are arranged in parallel and have independent exits to the exterior. The west façade, dominated by the lounge, dining room and study, is an exquisite exercise in simplicity. A window emerges from the master bedroom at eye level, and rips open the walls in a daring yet fragile flourish of beauty. The inner courtyard challenges these façades for attention, however, opening at the level of the entrance and dividing the main façades into two clearly defined areas: one contains the nocturnal areas of the house, while the other is given over to the remaining bedrooms and the garden.

Cette maison, conçue comme une habitation familiale pour un couple avec trois enfants, est adaptée au terrain allongé et prend la forme d'un prisme dont les faces plus petites sont occupées par les façades principales, où se concentre la majorité des ouvertures et où se situent les chambres à coucher. La façade accueille les chambres à coucher des enfants, disposées parallèlement et pourvues d'accès indépendants depuis l'extérieur. La façade ouest, dominée par le salon, la salle à manger et le studio, est un exercice architectural d'une simplicité exquise. Une fenêtre située à hauteur de vue de l'observateur émerge de la chambre à coucher principale et déchire le mur, à l'instar d'une fioriture audacieuse à la beauté fragile. Le patio intérieur rivalise avec les façades principales pour attirer l'attention, s'ouvrant à la hauteur de l'entrée pour les diviser en deux zones clairement définies : l'une pour les zones de nuit, et l'autre accueillant les autres chambres et le jardin.

Dieses Familienhaus für ein Paar mit drei Kindern steht auf einem langen Grundstück mit der Form eines Prismas, dessen kleinere Seiten von den Hauptfassaden eingenommen werden. Dort befinden sich die meisten Fenster und die Schlafzimmer. Im Ostteil liegen die Kinderzimmer, die parallel angeordnet sind und jeweils einen unabhängigen Zugang haben. Im Westen liegen das Wohnzimmer, das Speisezimmer und das Atelier, alles einfach und stilvoll gehalten. Das Fenster auf Augenhöhe im Elternschlafzimmer wirkt wie ein Dekorationsgegenstand mit zerbrechlicher Schönheit. Der Innenhof zieht ebenso wie die Fassaden die Aufmerksamkeit auf sich. Er öffnet sich auf Höhe des Eingangs und unterteilt die Hauptfassaden in zwei klar definierte Bereiche, hinter einer liegen die Bereiche für die Nacht, hinter der anderen die übrigen Zimmer und der Garten.

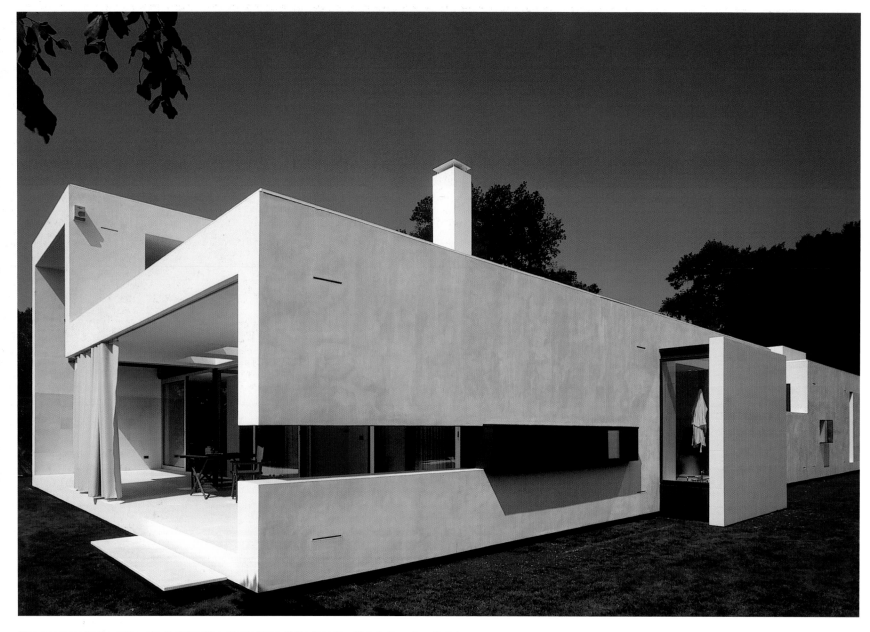

The openings in the side walls highlight the simple lines of the façade without disrupting their harmony.

Les creux des murs latéraux rehaussent, sans en rompre l'harmonie, la simplicité des lignes de la façade.

Die Öffnungen an den Seitenwänden unterstreichen die Einfachheit der Fassade, ohne die Harmonie zu zerstören.

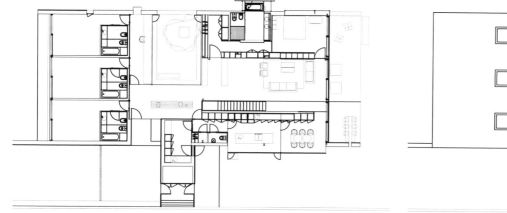

› **First floor** Premier étage Erstes Obergeschoss

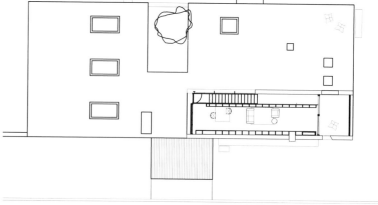

› **Second floor** Deuxième étage Zweites Obergeschoss

The floors, walls and roof are finished in the same material, as is the terrace, and it penetrates into the interior until reaching a glass panel.

Le même revêtement se retrouve sur le sol, les murs et la couverture, y compris la terrasse, et à l'intérieur, il s'étend jusqu'à un panneau de verre.

Am Boden, an den Wänden und an der Decke wurde die gleiche Verkleidung benutzt. Sie ist auch auf der Terrasse zu finden und dringt bis ins Innere.

The bedrooms are located behind the main façade, which has the greatest number of openings.

Les chambres sont situées sur la façade principale, dotée de la majorité des ouvertures.

Die Schlafzimmer befinden sich an der Hauptfassade, wo die meisten Fenster sind.

Light flows through the various spaces in the house by means of the numerous openings, such as the skylight above the bath or the glass blocks on the top floor.

La lumière afflue des différents espaces à travers de nombreuses ouvertures, à l'instar de la lucarne qui illumine la baignoire ou les blocs de verre du dernier étage.

Das Licht fällt durch zahlreiche Fenster in die Räume, uns so wird durch ein Dachfenster die Badewanne beschienen.

Schmitz House
Maison Schmitz
Haus Schmitz

Calera de Tango, Chile

The commission for this project, located in the Andes on the Chilean coast, entailed designing a house in the middle of an orchard for a couple without children. The final design rises a concrete box one 3.3 feet tall and 6.6 feet wide, pointing east to west, that would house the pool and basement, and would also serve as the foundation for the house. The ground floor was situated above this platform, at the height of the branches of the fruit trees: it is a glass and larch box that holds all the common areas in a single diaphanous space whose only enclosures conceal the bathroom and the guest bedroom. The upper floor, designed in exposed concrete, sits perpendicularly atop this ensemble. The house's north-south orientation means that part of the upper floor projects out in cantilever and casts small areas of the lower façade into shadow. The living room walls are entirely made of glass and the master bedroom was designed to be predominantly opaque.

Dans ce projet, situé dans les Andes, les montagnes le long de la côte chilienne, il s'agissait de concevoir une maison au milieu d'un champ d'arbres fruitiers pour un couple sans enfants. Cette maison est conçue à partir d'un bloc de béton d'un mètre de haut et de 2,7 m de large, orienté est-ouest qui accueille la piscine, le sous-sol et qui en même temps sert de fondations. Au-dessus, le rez-de-chaussée est implanté au niveau de la cime des arbres : un volume conjuguant verre et bois de mélèze qui abrite les zones communes réparties sur un espace unique diaphane que l'on peut fermer uniquement pour masquer les salles de bains et une chambre d'amis. Installé perpendiculairement à l'ensemble, le premier étage est en béton apparent. Dû à sa situation nord-sud, il est construit partiellement en saillie, sculptant ainsi des petites ombres sur les façades inférieures. Le salon est entièrement vitré alors que dans la chambre à coucher principale, c'est l'opaque qui prédomine.

Dieses Haus zwischen den Anden und den Bergen an der Küste von Chile wurde inmitten eines Feldes voller Obstbäume für ein kinderloses Paar entworfen. Es wurde ein ein Meter hoher und 2,7 Meter breiter Betonkasten konstruiert, der in Richtung Westen zeigt und in dem sich der Swimmingpool und der Keller befinden und der gleichzeitig das Fundament des Hauses ist. Auf Höhe der Baumkronen wurde das Erdgeschoss angelegt, eine Konstruktion aus Glas und Lärche, in dem die Gemeinschaftsbereiche in einem einzigen, transparenten Raum liegen, der nur geschlossen wird, um die Bäder und das Gästezimmer zu verbergen. Die obere Ebene des senkrecht angelegten Baus besteht aus unverputztem Beton. Durch die Nord-Südlage befindet sich dieses Stockwerk auf einem Vorsprung, so dass kleine Schatten auf die unteren Fassaden fallen. Das Wohnzimmer ist vollständig verglast und das Hauptschlafzimmer ist zum größten Teil undurchsichtig angelegt.

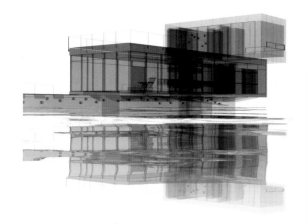

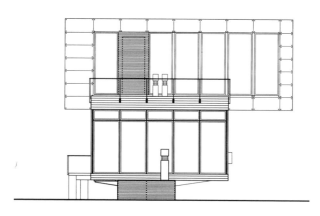

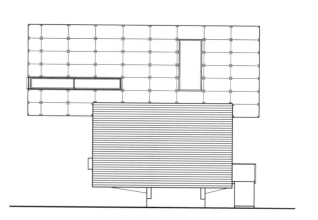

› Elevations Élévations Aufrisse

The foundation walls also serve as the load-bearing walls for the swimming pool, which is surrounded by a dark-colored wooden deck.

Les fondations servent de murs de soutènement de la piscine entourée d'une terrasse recouverte en lattes de bois foncé.

Die Fundamente wurden als Staumauern für den Swimmingpool benutzt, der von einer mit dunklen Holzlatten belegten Terrasse umgeben ist.

Cabinets are located on both sides of the kitchen supported by slender metal columns.

Le meuble de la cuisine est composé de deux blocs d'armoires soutenus grâce à des piliers métalliques élancés.

Das Küchenmöbel besteht aus zwei gestreiften Schränke, die von schlanken Metallpfeilern gehalten werden.

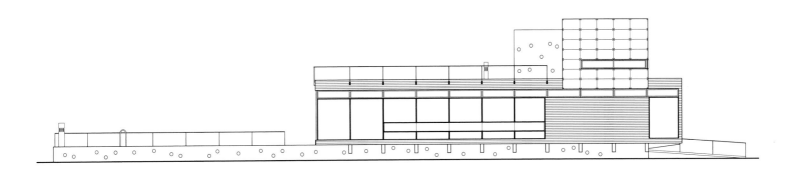

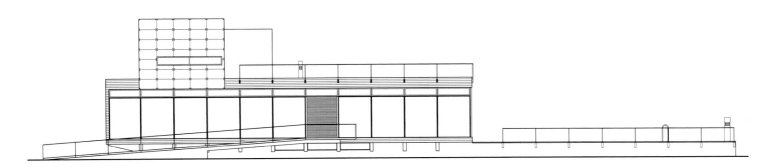

› Elevations Élévations Aufrisse

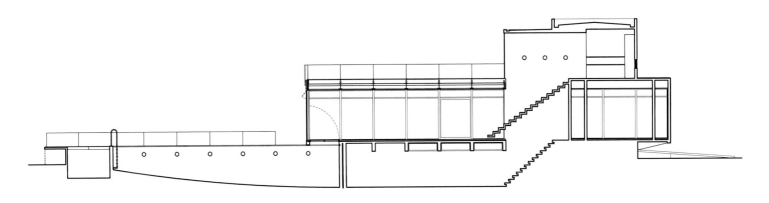

› Longitudinal section Section longitudinale Längsschnitt

Crescent House
Maison Crescent
Crescent Haus

Wiltshire, UK

Before they started on the design of this house, Ken and Seana Shuttleworth established a framework for it: they needed an ample and light-filled space that would be both functional and committed to the landscape around it. A large curving wall accompanies the visitor, leading the way to the house and drawing one's gaze to a stunning garden. All of the private spaces are located in the semicircle facing northeast, which was made opaque to protect the house from the wind and the gaze of onlookers. The bedrooms, bathrooms and dressing rooms occupy small, contemplative spaces, lit from above. The semicircle facing southeast looks out onto the garden, which can be seen throughout the house thanks to the glass façade. The dining room, kitchen and living room occupy a single continuous space with 10 feet ceilings, which is inundated with natural light and directly connected to the natural surroundings.

Avant d'initier leur projet de maison, Ken y Seana Shuttleworth ont posé les idées directrices de la conception de leur futur foyer : un espace généreux et lumineux, fonctionnel et adapté au lieu. Un grand mur, tout en courbes, guide le visiteur en sublimant l'accès et en faisant dévier les regards vers le magnifique jardin. Tous les espaces privés sont situés dans l'hémicycle orienté au nord-est, conçu dans une matière opaque pour protéger du vent et des regards indiscrets. Les chambres à coucher, les salles de bains et les dressings occupent des petites pièces ravissantes qui reçoivent la lumière zénithale. Le demi-cercle orienté au sud-est s'ouvre sur le jardin grâce à une façade entièrement vitrée. La salle à manger, la cuisine et le salon occupent un espace unique et continu de 3,5 m de hauteur, inondé de lumière naturelle et directement relié à la nature environnante.

Bevor sie mit der Planung begannen, definierten Ken und Seana Shuttleworth, wie ihr künftiges Heim aussehen sollte. Ein weiter und heller Raum, funktionell und mit der Umgebung in Harmonie. Eine große, gebogene Mauer begleitet den Besucher und führt ihn zum Eingang, gleichzeitig lenkt sie den Blick auf den wundervollen Garten. Alle Privaträume befinden sich im nordwestlichen, massiv konstruierten Halbkreis, so dass weder der Wind noch unerwünschte Blicke eindringen können. Die Schlafzimmer, Bäder und Ankleidezimmer sind kleine, ruhige Räume mit Deckenlicht. Im südöstlichen Halbkreis hat man einen Blick auf den Garten und die Fassade ist vollständig verglast. Das Esszimmer, die Küche und das Wohnzimmer befinden sich in einem einzigen, durchgehenden, 3,5 m hohen Raum, in den großzügig Tageslicht einfällt und der die umgebende Natur miteinbezieht.

The house opens onto a spectacular garden to the southeast. The large glass façade blurs the perception of a boundary between interior and exterior.

La maison s'ouvre sur un splendide jardin situé au sud-est. La grande façade de verre atténue la limite entre l'intérieur et l'extérieur de l'habitation.

Das Haus öffnet sich auf einen wundervollen Garten im Südosten. Die große verglaste Fassade lässt die Grenze zwischen innen und außen verschwinden.

Pale colors dominate in all the finishes, floors, walls and furniture, so as to fill the home with light.

La dominance des tons clairs des finitions, sols, murs et du mobilier exalte la luminosité intérieure.

Helle Farben dominieren an den Oberflächen, Böden, Wänden und Möbeln. Dadurch wirken die Räume noch heller.

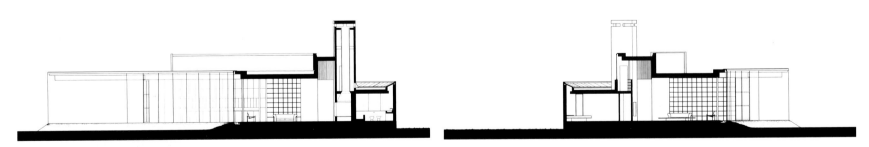

› Sections Sections Schnitte

No trees were cut down to build the house and over one thousand were planted in order to foster a microclimate that reduces energy consumption.

Aucun arbre n'a été abattu et plus de mille arbres ont été plantés pour créer un microclimat permettant de réduire la dépense d'énergie de la maison.

Es wurde kein Baum gefällt und über Tausende gepflanzt, um ein energiesparendes Mikroklima zu schaffen.

Furniture-House
Maison-meuble
Möbel-Haus

Yamanaka, Japan

In order to build this house in accordance with the extreme simplicity of the Orient, its architect designed its structure around partitions and a storage area. The house was built using prefabricated furniture units that stretch to the ceiling and function structurally as elements that define the space. Each individual prefabricated unit, which weighs approximately 177 pounds, can easily be manipulated by one person. The six strips of structural furniture, which are used as screens to subdivide the space, create different zones within one continuous space. The architect arranged the elements so that their layout would direct the viewer's gaze towards a large platform, while the large windows, which slide along rails hidden in the floor and the ceiling, link the space in the house with the surrounding landscape.

Pour placer la conception de cette maison sous le signe d'une extrême simplicité orientale, l'architecte en a conçu la structure à partir des cloisons et de la zone domestique. Le système de construction est basé sur des unités de mobilier préfabriquées déterminant la hauteur totale de l'édifice et dont les éléments de structure définissent l'espace : une unité individuelle préfabriquée, pesant environ quatre-vingt kilos et facilement manœuvrable par une seule personne. Les six unités de meubles de structure, utilisés comme des cloisons, créent différentes zones au sein d'un espace fluide. L'architecte a simplement placé les éléments pour que les tensions orientent le mouvement et le regard vers la plate-forme, alors que les grandes fenêtres coulissantes sur des rails masqués dans le sol et le toit, contribuent à établir le lien entre l'espace de la maison et le paysage environnant.

Dieses Haus wurde in einem extrem einfachen fern östlichen Stil geplant, wobei der Architekt seine Struktur an die Aufteilungen und den Lagerbereich anpasste. Die Konstruktion basiert auf vorgefertigten Möbeleinheiten, die die Höhe des Gebäudes bestimmen und strukturell als Elemente funktionieren, die den Raum definieren. Eine individuelle, vorgefertigte Einheit, die ungefähr 80 Kilo wiegt, kann leicht von einer einzigen Person bewegt werden. Die sechs Streifen mit Strukturmöbeln, die als Trennwände dienen, schaffen verschiedene Bereiche in einem einzigen, durchgehenden Raum. Der Architekt stellt einfach die Elemente auf, damit die Spannungen die Bewegung und den Blick zu einer großen Plattform leiten. Die großen Fenster gleiten auf im Boden und in der Decke verborgenen Schienen, so dass der Wohnraum mit der umgebenden Landschaft verbunden wird.

This system allowed the designer to achieve the desired degree of refinement and to have a minimal impact on the natural environment, even during the construction phase.

Ce système permet d'atteindre le degré de dépouillement désiré avec une incidence minimale sur l'environnement naturel y compris sur le déroulement de la phase de construction.

Durch dieses System wird der gewünschte Grad an Reinheit erreicht und es beeinflusst die umgebende Natur kaum. Schon in der Bauphase wurde die Natur sehr schonend behandelt.

The boundaries between the areas of circulation and the living areas are practically non-existent, or are very subtly marked.

Les limites entre les espaces de circulation et les pièces à vivre sont pratiquement inexistantes et sont définies tout en subtilité.

Es existieren praktisch keine Grenzen zwischen den Wohnbereichen und den Durchgängen, sie werden nur subtil angedeutet.

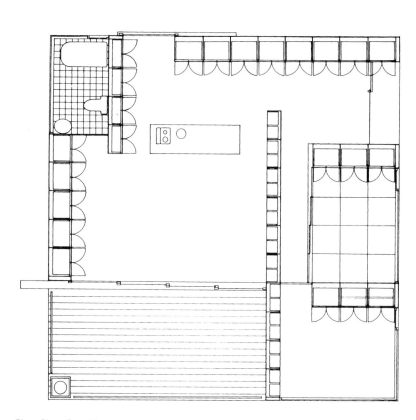

› Plan Plan Grundriss

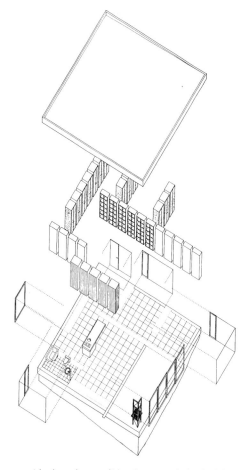

› Axonometric view Axonométrie Axonometrische Ansicht

The shelves are organized in accordance with the structure and composition of the bedrooms by exercising vertical and horizontal tension.

Les pièces s'organisent en fonction de la structure et de la composition des chambres, en exerçant des tensions verticales et horizontales.

Die Regale sind der Struktur und Gestaltung der Zimmer entsprechend organisiert und verursachen eine vertikale oder horizontale Spannung.

Mediterranean Dwelling
Habitation méditerranéenne
Mediterranes Wohnhaus

Milan, Italy

This rectangular home, located in an industrial area was built on the site of a demolished building, which served as the volumetric model for its replacement. The structure of the patio—typical of Roman and Mediterranean houses—was maintained, even though the new building does display interventions done in a more contemporary vein. The house was conceived of as being completely open to an extensive garden—which was achieved through the use of sliding glass doors. Likewise, to take advantage of natural daylight, all the bedrooms open on to it. The home is structured around three main areas: the service area, the daytime area and a nocturnal area. The main entrance leads to the living room, which is 33 feet long and stretches into the indoor courtyard. The succession of different spaces guarantees a unique vista from any corner of the house.

De plan rectangulaire, cette habitation, située dans une zone industrielle, s'élève à la place d'une construction démolie dont elle s'inspire pour ses volumes. La structure du patio, typique des maisons romaines et méditerranéennes, a été conservée, même si le nouvel édifice présente aussi des traits d'architecture contemporaine. La maison s'ouvre complètement sur le grand jardin -conception réalisée grâce à un système de portes en verre coulissantes- avec toutes les chambres qui donnent sur cet univers de verdure, profitant ainsi de la lumière naturelle du jour. L'habitation s'articule autour de trois espaces principaux : domestique, de jour et de nuit. L'entrée principale mène jusqu'au salon, long de dix mètres environ et qui s'étend jusqu'au patio intérieur. L'enfilade des différentes sphères crée une seule perspective depuis n'importe quel point de l'habitation.

Dieses Wohnhaus mit rechteckigem Grundriss steht in einem Industriegebiet auf einem Grundstück, auf dem ein Gebäude abgerissen wurde, das jedoch als Modell für den Neubau diente. Die Struktur des Hofes, die typisch für römische und mediterrane Häuser ist, wurde beibehalten. Jedoch weist das neue Gebäude auch architektonische Eingriffe im zeitgenössischen Stil auf. Das Haus wurde mithilfe von gläsernen Schiebetüren vollständig offen zu dem großen Garten hin angelegt. Alle Zimmer liegen zu diesem Garten, und das Tageslicht erhellt alle Räume. Das Wohnhaus gliedert sich in drei Hauptbereiche auf, einen funktionellen Bereich, eine Zone für den Tag und eine für die Nacht. Der Haupteingang führt zum Wohnzimmer, das ungefähr zehn Meter lang ist und sich bis zum Innenhof erstreckt. Die verschiedenen Wohnumgebungen folgen einander, wodurch eine einzigartige Perspektive von jedem Punkt des Hauses aus entsteht.

From the dining room and the kitchen, there is an unusual view of the pool, which is transformed into a decorative and functional element.

Depuis la salle à manger et la cuisine, la perspective inhabituelle sur la piscine en fait un élément décoratif et fonctionnel.

Vom Esszimmer und der Küche aus hat man einen Blick auf den Swimmingpool, der zu einem dekorativen und funktionellen Element wird.

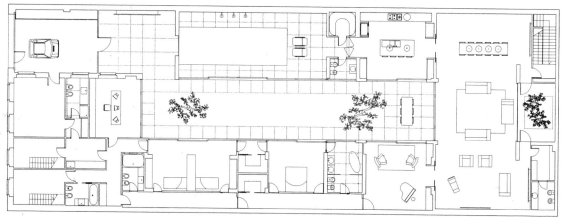

› Plan Plan Grundriss

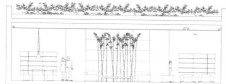

› Cross section   Section transversale   Querschnitt

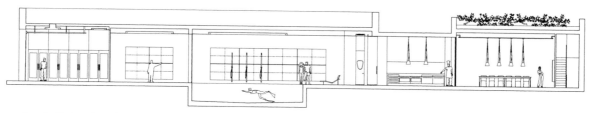

› Longitudinal section   Section longitudinale   Längsschnitt

House on Iritahama Beach
Habitation sur la plage de Iritahama
Haus am Strand von Iritahama

Shizuoka, Japan

The location, distinguished by a sloping terrain, offers this house luxurious views of Iritahama Beach, which is considered to be one of the most beautiful in all of Japan. The main challenge in designing this house was to maintain the 270° panoramic views which explains the practically transparent enclosure-while still protecting it from typhoons, the sun and the gaze of onlookers. The foundation of the house was built with screens of reinforced concrete to lend rigidity to the platform upon which the rest of the house lies, and a covering of perforated slats was attached to metal rails to span the length of the façade. This system can be manipulated to vary the amount of light that can filter in and at the same time to protect the house in bad weather.

La situation privilégiée que l'inclinaison du terrain confère à cette habitation, lui offre des vues splendides sur la plage de Iritahama, considérée comme étant une des plus belles de tout le Japon. Le principal défi conceptuel était de réussir à ce que l'édifice préserve l'angle de vue de 270° offert par l'enclave - obtenu par un écran pratiquement transparent - et en même temps le protéger des typhons, du soleil et des regards indiscrets. Le système de construction comporte des fondations à base de panneaux de béton armé qui rendent la structure rigide et qui soutiennent une plate-forme sur laquelle le reste de l'édifice s'appuie et une coque de plaques perforées montées sur rails métalliques tout le long de la façade. Ce système permet de moduler la filtration de la lumière et sert en même temps de protection contre les intempéries.

Dieses Haus steht auf einem Grundstück mit einem schönen Blick auf den Strand von Iritahama, vielleicht einer der schönsten von ganz Japan. Ziel der Planung war es, den Sichtwinkel von 270°, den es auf dem Grundstück gab, beizubehalten, weshalb die Mauern fast transparent sind, aber dennoch das Haus vor Taifunen, der Sonne und indiskreten Blicken zu schützen. Das Haus besitzt ein Fundament aus verschiedenen Abschirmungen aus Stahlbeton, die der Struktur Festigkeit geben und eine Plattform halten, auf der das übrige Gebäude steht. Die gesamte Fassade ist mit gelochten Platten verkleidet, die auf Metallschienen montiert sind. Diese Verkleidung kann eingestellt werden, um verschiedene Lichtmengen einzulassen und vor ungünstigen Wetterbedingungen zu schützen.

To the right, a perforated slat allows for the façade of the house to be completely closed to protect it from strong winds.

A droite, la plaque perforée permet de fermer complètement la façade de la maison pour la protéger des vents violents.

Auf der rechten Seite kann man mit einer gelochten Platte die Fassade des Hauses vollständig schließen, um sie vor Wind zu schützen.

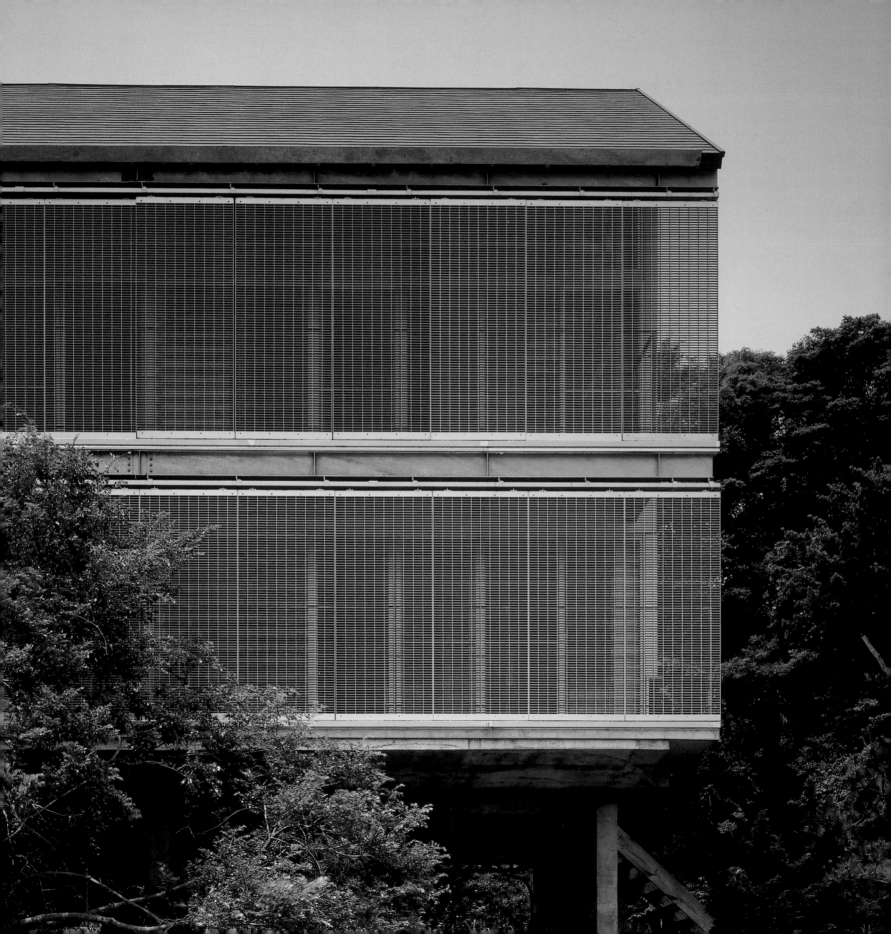

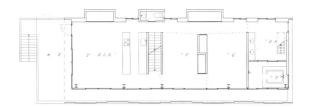

› Ground floor Rez-de-chaussée Erdgeschoss

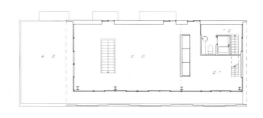

› First floor Premier étage Erstes Obergeschoss

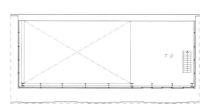

› Second floor Deuxième étage Zweites Obergeschoss

The main sitting room was designed as an open and continuous space that offers panoramic views of Iritahama Beach.

Le salon principal se présente comme un espace ouvert et fluide qui jouit de la vue panoramique sur la plage de Iritahama.

Das Wohnzimmer ist ein offener und durchgehender Raum, von dem aus man einen Panoramablick auf den Strand von Iritahama hat.

The sitting room was conceived as a diaphanous space with furnishings, thus favoring a visual relationship with the surrounding area.

Le salon est conçu comme un espace diaphane, minimaliste sur le plan du mobilier, choix qui favorise la communication visuelle avec l'espace environnant.

Das Wohnzimmer ist ein durchscheinender Raum mit wenig Möbeln, so dass die visuelle Kommunikation mit der Umgebung verstärkt wird.

Eremo Residence
Résidence Eremo
Haus Eremo

Cuneo, Italy

This one-story, rectangular house is located in a breathtaking landscape with the Alps as its backdrop. As it is nestled on a high hill, this house enjoys unbeatable views. The distribution of the interior is linear: the kitchen and the lounge are located at one end, with access to the bedroom and service areas. A curving stone wall and a wooden bed suspended from the ceiling by steel cables are two of the elements that stand out in this otherwise neutral and relaxing home. The materials used in the house illustrate the dialogue between structure and landscape; natural components such as wood and stone are used in different ways and are present both inside and out.

Cette habitation est située dans un paysage évocateur et grandiose avec les Alpes pour cadre. Située en haut d'une colline, cette construction rectangulaire est d'un seul niveau et peut tirer parti de la singularité du site. La distribution intérieure est linéaire : la cuisine et le salon, situés à une des extrémités, sont contigus à la salle à manger qui permet d'accéder aux chambres et aux zones de service. Un mur de pierre cintré et un lit suspendu au toit par des câbles d'acier sont les deux éléments qui se détachent de ce logis neutre et décontracté. Le choix des matériaux laisse transparaître le dialogue de la structure avec l'environnement : les composantes naturelles à l'instar du bois et de la pierre, sont employées de différentes manières et se retrouvent tant à l'extérieur qu'à l'intérieur.

Dieses Wohnhaus befindet sich in einer wunderschönen Gegend am Fuße der Alpen. Es liegt auf einem Hügel, ist nur ein Stockwerk hoch und rechteckig angelegt, und die umgebende Landschaft macht es einzigartig. Innen sind die Räume linear verteilt, die Küche und das Wohnzimmer befinden sich an einem Ende, es folgt das Esszimmer, von dem aus man die Schlafzimmer und die funktionellen Bereiche betritt. Eine gekrümmte Steinwand und ein Holzbett, das mit Stahlkabeln an der Decke aufgehängt ist, sind zwei der Elemente, die in dieser neutral und ruhig wirkenden Wohnumgebung auffallen. Durch die Auswahl der Materialien entstand ein Dialog zwischen der Struktur und der Umgebung. Natürliche Komponenten wie Holz und Stein werden auf verschiedene Arten verwendet und sind sowohl innen als auch außen anzutreffen.

The façade opens on to the garden and combines aluminium, glass and local stone to lend expressiveness to the ensemble.

La façade s'ouvre sur le jardin, et en associant l'aluminium, le verre et la pierre de la région, donne du caractère à l'ensemble.

Die Fassade öffnet sich zum Garten. Die Kombination von Aluminium, Glas und Steinen aus der Umgebung verleihen dem Gebäude einen besonderen Charakter.

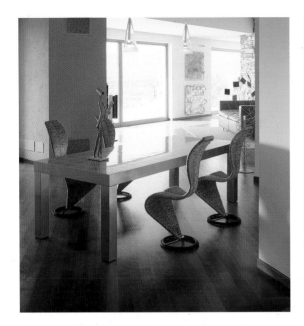

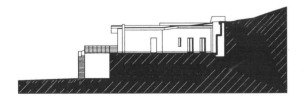

› Cross section   Section transversale   Querschnitt

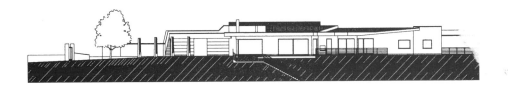

› Longitudinal section   Section longitudinale   Längsschnitt

The interior is designed to take advantage of the stunning views and to achieve a maximum visual connection with the outdoors.

L'intérieur est conçu pour profiter des vues privilégiées, créant ainsi le maximum de lien visuel avec l'extérieur.

Aus den Räumen hat man einen wundervollen Ausblick und es besteht eine starke, visuelle Verbindung zwischen Innen und Außen.

Residence in Pacific Palisades
Résidence à Pacific Palisades
Haus in Pacific Palisades

Los Angeles, USA

Designed in 1949 by Richard Neutra for screenwriters Benedict and Nancy Freedman, this complex emerges atop a vast site and enjoys spectacular views of the sea. Between 1959 and 1988, a number of different architects carried out additions to the house. Studio Bau:ton was at the helm during the mid-1990s, and over the space of the next ten years completed the shed, fence, doors, entry stairs and the overall design of the garden. A reflecting pool was built next to the entrance and the fence was also repainted in its original ruddy color. From 1999 to 2002, a second floor was added, with two bedrooms and bathrooms, the main bedroom was enlarged and the kitchen was remodelled. These new incorporations were blended into the original structure, and the basic idea of unimpeded flow between interior and exterior was both maintained and reinforced throughout the house.

Conçu en 1949 par Richard Neutra pour les scénaristes Benedict et Nancy Freedman, ce complexe est implanté sur un grand terrain et jouit de vues privilégiées sur la mer. Entre 1959 et 1988 divers architectes ajoutèrent certains éléments. Le studio Bau:ton s'est chargé du projet au milieu des années quatre-vingt et durant cette décennie, les éléments extérieurs manquant furent terminés : auvent, barrières, portes, escaliers d'entrée et conception générale du jardin. Un étang a été placé à côté de l'entrée et les barrières ont retrouvé leur aspect original en bois peint rouge. De 1999 à 2002, l'addition d'un second étage a été entreprise, accueillant deux chambres à coucher et des salles de bains, ainsi que l'agrandissement de la salle de bains principale et la réhabilitation de la cuisine. Les nouveaux éléments se mêlèrent à la structure d'origine, et l'idée de base d'une ouverture fluide entre l'intérieur et l'extérieur a été maintenue et accentuée dans toutes les zones.

Dieser 1949 von Richard Neutra für die Drehbuchautoren Benedict und Nancy Freedman entworfene Gebäudekomplex steht auf einem großen Grundstück mit einem wundervollen Blick aufs Meer. Zwischen 1959 und 1988 fügten mehrere Architekten neue Anbauten hinzu. Das Studio Bau:ton übernahm dieses Projekt Mitte der Neunzigerjahre und in dieser Dekade wurden die fehlenden äußeren Elemente ergänzt, ein Vordach, Abdeckungen, Türen, Eingangstreppen und die Gartengestaltung. Es wurde auch ein Teich am Eingang angelegt und die Abdeckungen aus rötlich gestrichenem Holz restauriert. Zwischen 1999 und 2002 wurde ein zweites Geschoss mit Schlafzimmern und Bädern errichtet, das Hauptbad wurde erweitert und die Küche umgebaut. Die neuen Anbauten mischen sich mit der Originalstruktur. Es sollte ein fließender Übergang zwischen Innen und Außen überall im Gebäude entstehen.

Although the house was renovated in a gradual fashion over the years, the spirit of continuity through the generations has not been lost.

La restauration de la résidence s'est faite progressivement, au fil des années, sans nuire à l'esprit de continuité entre les différentes générations.

Das Haus wurde allmählich im Laufe der Jahre umgebaut, was jedoch den Geist der Kontinuität zwischen den verschiedenen Generationen nicht beeinträchtigt hat.

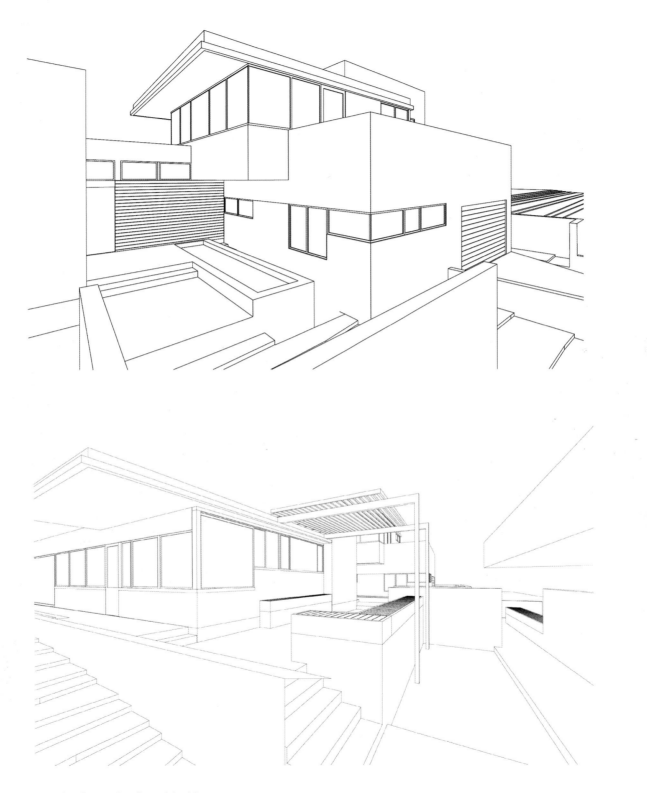

› Perspective Perspective Perspektivzeichnung

In some parts of the house, the renovation included new pieces of furniture that comprised integral parts of the structure.

Dans certaines parties de l'habitation, le concept de restauration inclut le choix d'éléments de mobilier, qui sont parties intégrantes de la structure.

In einigen Teilen des Hauses wurden neue Möbel als Bestandteil der Struktur aufgenommen.

The dense structure of the house contrasts with the open garden that slopes down towards the Pacific, which can be seen from the living room through a series of large windows.

La grande densité structurelle contraste avec le jardin ouvert qui se tourne vers l'océan, visible depuis le salon grâce à de larges baies vitrées.

Die große strukturelle Dichte steht zu dem offenen Garten im Gegensatz, der sich zum Meer hin neigt, das man vom Wohnzimmer aus durch große Fenster sehen kann.

Set aside in a nook on the ground floor, a shower totally open to the garden allows one to bathe amidst the tranquillity of nature.

Au rez-de-chaussée, située dans un espace protégé, une douche totalement ouverte sur le terrain permet de s'arroser dans le calme qui émane de ce lieu.

Im Erdgeschoss befindet sich in einer dafür gestalteten Zone eine Dusche, die ganz zum Garten hin geöffnet ist. Hier kann man die Ruhe des Ortes genießen.

Chalet in Lissago
Pavillon à Lissago
Chalet in Lissago

Lissago, Italy

The objective of the renovation of this house was to achieve a maximum influx of light by means of a structure made up of linear forms. Deliberate cuts were made in the inside walls, some of which establish a relationship with the exterior and others which create links between the various spaces of the house. The stairs serve as the central element of the public area, and the kitchen was built in a strategically chosen location with views of the children's bedroom and the garden. A partition separates the stairs from the dining room, which is open to the living room. To foster a visual connection with the exterior, the floor of the porch was made of wooden slats and is bathed in light from above thanks to a series of large skylights. From the porch, one can enjoy a pleasant view of the garden and the pool, which is surrounded by a deck crafted in iroko wood.

Cette habitation a été restaurée dans le but d'obtenir un maximum de lumière grâce à une structure aux formes linéaires. Les murs intérieurs ont été pourvus d'ouvertures soigneusement étudiées, les unes pour établir un lien avec l'extérieur et les autres pour relier les divers espaces de la maison. L'escalier est l'élément central de la zone publique, et la cuisine, un lieu de séjour stratégique d'où l'on aperçoit la chambre des enfants et le jardin. Une cloison sépare les escaliers de la salle à manger reliée au salon. L'atrium est recouvert de boiseries et baigné de lumière zénithale grâce à des fenêtres de toit, accentuant ainsi le lien visuel avec l'extérieur. Cela permet d'avoir une vue agréable sur le jardin et la piscine, entourée d'un plancher de bois d'iroko.

Ziel der Renovierung dieses Wohnhauses war es, aus dem Licht ein wichtiges Gestaltungselement zu machen, was durch eine Struktur mit linearen Formen erreicht wurde. An den Innenwänden schuf man vorsichtig einige Öffnungen, von denen manche eine Beziehung zwischen außen und innen schaffen und andere die verschiedenen Bereiche der Wohnung miteinander verbinden. Die Treppe dient als zentrales Element für den Wohnbereich, die Küche befindet sich an einem strategischen Ort, von dem aus man das Kinderzimmer und den Garten sieht. Ein Raumteiler trennt die Treppe vom Esszimmer, das mit dem Wohnzimmer verbunden ist. Um die visuelle Verbindung nach draußen zu verbessern, wurde der Boden der Veranda mit Holz belegt und durch Dachfenster fällt viel Licht von oben auf diese Veranda ein. Von hier aus hat man einen schönen Blick auf den Garten und den Swimmingpool, der von einem Boden aus Iroko umgeben ist.

The most distinctive characteristics of this house are its spectacular garden and pool, which are visible from the porch.

Les caractéristiques notables de cette maison sont le jardin spectaculaire et sa piscine que l'on peut admirer depuis l'atrium.

Was dieses Haus so besonders macht, ist der wundervolle Garten mit dem Swimmingpool, den man von der Veranda aus genießen kann.

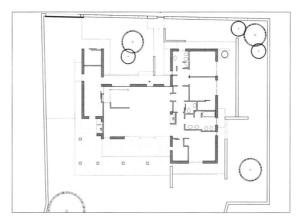

› Plan Plan Grundriss

Beech parquet was used to floor the dining room and the bedrooms. The living room and the dining room share one single open space.

Le parquet de la salle à manger et des chambres est en bois de hêtre. Le salon et la salle à manger se partagent le même espace ouvert.

Für die Fußböden des Esszimmers und der Schlafzimmer wurde Buchenparkett benutzt. Das Wohn- und Esszimmer befinden sich in einem einzigen, offenen Raum.

The kitchen is located directly behind the stairs and is completely separated from the living room.

La cuisine, située juste derrière l'escalier, est totalement séparée du salon.

Die Küche liegt genau hinter der Treppe und ist so völlig vom Wohnzimmer abgetrennt.

Tennessee River Residence
Résidence Tennessee River
Haus Tennessee River

Tennessee, USA

This house sits atop the edge of a dramatic cliff over the Tennessee River, to the east of Shiloh National Park. This peculiar enclave houses the owner's collections of contemporary photography and pre-Columbian art, in a building that detaches from the highest level and divides itself downward into three different levels. The living room and the dining room, as a final touch to the composition and in contrast with the previously linear scheme, are located in a double-height glass-lined space. The bedrooms are on the floor below, with a closer view of the surrounding trees and relax in greater intimacy. The materials chosen reinforce the general scheme of the house: brick at the base to adapt to the soil, glass surfaces and galvanized aluminium for the roof.

Cette construction surplombe une forte pente qui s'évanouit dans le fleuve Tennessee, à l'est du Parc National de Shiloh. C'est une enclave qui héberge les collections de photographie contemporaine et d'art précolombien du propriétaire, dans un édifice qui se décroche de la partie supérieure du terrain pour se diviser en trois niveaux distincts. Le salon et la salle à manger, point d'orgue de la construction, contrastant avec le schéma linéaire antérieur, s'inscrivent dans un espace entièrement vitré sur deux hauteurs. Les chambres sont situées au niveau inférieur qui offre une vue plus proche de la nature créant ainsi une atmosphère plus intime et protégée. Les matériaux exaltent le schéma global de la maison : base en briques épousant le terrain, superficies de verre et d'aluminium galvanisé pour la couverture.

Dieses Haus steht am Rand eines steilen Hangs, der sich zum Fluss Tennessee im Osten des Nationalparks Shiloh neigt. An diesem besonderen Ort wurden die Sammlungen zeitgenössischer Fotografie und präkolumbischer Kunst des Besitzers untergebracht. Das Gebäude neigt sich vom höchsten Teil des Grundstücks herunter und teilt sich in drei Ebenen auf. Das Wohn- und Esszimmer wurden als Abschluss der Komposition und im Gegensatz zu dem vorherigen linearen Schema als ein verglaster Raum doppelter Höhe angelegt. Die Schlafzimmer befinden sich im untersten Stockwerk, wo man einen besseren Blick auf die Vegetation hat. Dadurch wird hier die Atmosphäre intimer und geschützter. Das allgemeine Konzept des Hauses wird durch die Materialien unterstrichen, Ziegelstein im unteren Bereich, der sich an den Boden anpasst, am Dach Flächen aus Glas und galvanisierten Aluminium.

The site is located on a cliff 120 feet up from the west bank of the river, which grants it an unequalled panoramic view.

Le terrain est situé à 36 mètres au-dessus du niveau de l'eau sur le côté est de la falaise, offrant une vue panoramique incomparable.

Das Grundstück liegt 36 Meter über dem Wasserspiegel im Westen der Schlucht, so dass man einen phantastischen Panoramablick hat.

The longitudinal flow extends throughout the house until reaching the living room, which is perched right at the edge of the cliff.

Le schéma longitudinal s'étend tout le long de la façade pour s'arrêter au salon, juste au bord de la falaise.

Entlang des gesamten Gebäudes verläuft ein Weg, der bis zum Wohnzimmer direkt neben der Schlucht führt.

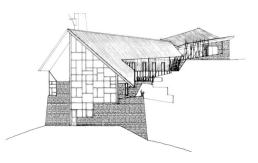

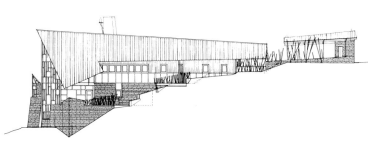

› Elevations Élévations Aufrisse

Bassil Residence
Résidence Bassil
Haus Bassil

Faqra, Lebanon

The idea behind this second residence was to provide a getaway for leisure activities and relaxation, as the client sought a peaceful environment to escape to periodically. The structure is defined by two superimposed cubes that share a single axis but intersect it at slightly different angles. One of the cubes is made of glass, while the other is made of stone. The lightness of the interior is reflected in the large, two-storey glass box, which offers spectacular views. The lower level houses the dining room and a terrace, and the second floor, a living room and the master bedroom. In the hall, an expansive, double-height window confronts the visitor with a panoramic view. This configuration also allows light to flood into all the rooms, especially the living room, which enjoys a prime location. The tinted glass softens the harsh sunlight of the area as it enters the house, and protects the interior from both extreme temperatures and unwanted glances.

La conception de cette résidence secondaire repose sur des critères de loisir et de détente, selon le désir du client qui cherchait un environnement paisible pour y passer certaines époques de l'année. La structure architecturale est composée de deux cubes superposés, sur un axe identique mais sous un angle différent : l'un est en verre et l'autre en pierre. La légèreté de l'intérieur se reflète dans la grande boîte de verre de deux niveaux offrant des vues spectaculaires. Le rez-de-chaussée héberge la salle à manger et une terrasse, et le deuxième étage accueille un salon et la chambre à coucher principale. Dans l'atrium, une grande baie vitrée sur deux hauteurs place le visiteur devant l'horizon lointain. Cette configuration permet aussi à la lumière d'inonder toutes les chambres, spécialement le salon, qui occupe un lieu privilégié. Les verres teintés amortissent l'intensité solaire de la région et protègent l'intérieur des hautes températures et des regards indiscrets.m

Die grundlegenden Konzepte für die Planung dieses Zweithauses waren Freizeit und Entspannung, da der Kunde eine ruhige Umgebung für bestimmte Zeiten im Jahr suchte. Die architektonische Struktur besteht aus zwei übereinander gelagerten Würfeln mit einer Achse, die jedoch eine unterschiedliche Ausrichtung haben. Einer der Würfel ist aus Glas und der andere aus Stein. Die Leichtigkeit des Inneren wird von dem großen, verglasten, zweistöckigen Kasten reflektiert, von dem aus man einen wundervollen Ausblick hat. Im Erdgeschoss befinden sich das Esszimmer und die Terrasse, im ersten Stock ein Wohnzimmer und das Hauptschlafzimmer. Im Eingangsbereich erlaubt ein vom Boden bis zur Decke reichendes Fenster Blicke auf den entfernten Horizont. So kann das Licht alle Zimmer und vor allem das Wohnzimmer erreichen. Die getönten Gläser dämpfen das intensive Sonnenlicht und schützen die Räume vor allzu hohen Temperaturen.

A glass prism appears to float before the pool, and thus transmits the sensation of lightness that the architect sought to convey.

Un prisme de verre semble flotter devant la piscine, et transmet la sensation de légèreté cherchée par l'architecte dans ce projet.

Ein Prisma aus Glas scheint vor dem Swimmingpool zu schweben. Es lässt ein Gefühl von Leichtigkeit entstehen, ganz wie es der Architekt geplant hatte.

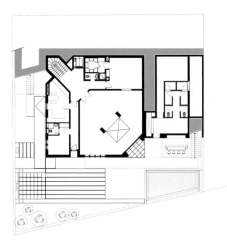

› Ground floor   Rez-de-chaussée   Erdgeschoss

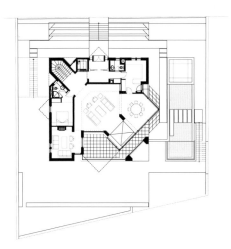

› First floor   Premier étage   Erstes Obergeschoss

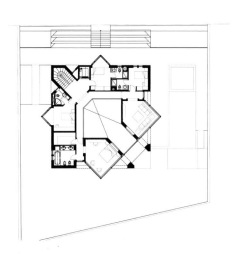

› Second floor   Deuxième étage   Zweites Obergeschoss

The garden is designed to create different meeting points and make the most of the landscape, as in this area next to the fireplace.

Le jardin est conçu pour générer des points de rencontre différents et tirer le meilleur parti du paysage, à l'instar de cette zone à proximité de la cheminée.

Im Garten gibt es verschiedene Treffpunkte. Die Landschaft wird in ihrer ganzen Schönheit gezeigt, so wie hier an der Fenerstelle.

Cutipol House
Maison Cutipol
Cutipol Haus

Guimarães, Portugal

In order to adapt this house to the specific characteristics of a highly uneven terrain, its architects focused on protecting the privacy of its occupants, even though doing so could affect the main façade of the house for the worse. The idea was to create as simple a shape as possible, with clearly defined lines and spaces that would blend in with the landscape. To achieve this, they designed a two-level volume that would adapt to the uneven ground, in such a way that the transition between the two would be linear. This unusual arrangement allowed them to open several parts of the house on to a series of terraces. The ground floor, on the lower part of the site, is joined to a large courtyard containing a semi-enclosed pool-this prevents sunlight from entering directly into the interior. A stairway leads to the upper floor, which houses the foyer, living room, bathrooms and bedrooms.

Pour adapter cette maison à un terrain très irrégulier, aux données particulières, les architectes ont choisi de privilégier les meilleures vues tout en protégeant l'intimité des habitants, même au détriment de la façade principale de la maison. Ils ont opté pour la forme la plus simple possible, aux lignes clairement définies, dotée d'espaces en harmonie avec le paysage environnant. Pour y parvenir, ils ont conçu un volume sur deux niveaux épousant la configuration du sol, créant ainsi une transition linéaire entre les deux. Cette disposition inhabituelle a permis d'ouvrir certaines parties de la maison sur les terrasses. Le rez-de-chaussée, situé en contre-bas de la pente, est réuni à un grand patio contenant une piscine semi-couverte, pour que le soleil ne puisse pénétrer directement à l'intérieur. Un escalier mène à l'étage supérieur où se trouve l'entrée de la maison, le salon, les salles de bains et les chambres à coucher.

Um dieses Haus an das sehr unregelmäßige Gelände anzupassen, haben sich die Architekten darauf konzentriert, für eine ausgezeichnete Aussicht und eine geschützte Intimsphäre zu sorgen, auch wenn sich dies negativ auf die Hauptfassade des Hauses auswirken sollte. Man wollte eine einfache Form schaffen, klar definierte Linien und Räume, die mit der umgebenden Landschaft im Einklang stehen. Dazu wurde ein Gebäude auf zwei Ebenen angelegt, das sich an die unregelmäßige Bodenform anpasst und so einen linearen Übergang schafft. Diese ungewöhnliche Aufteilung ermöglichte es, einige der Räume zu den Terrassen zu öffnen. Das Erdgeschoss, das am unteren Teil des Hangs liegt, führt zu einem großen Hof mit einem teilweise überdachten Swimmingpool, auf den die Sonne nicht direkt scheint. Eine Treppe führt zum Obergeschoss, in dem der Eingang, das Wohnzimmer, die Bäder und die Schlafzimmer liegen.

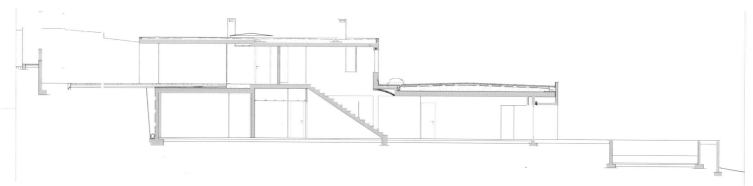

› Section Section Schnitt

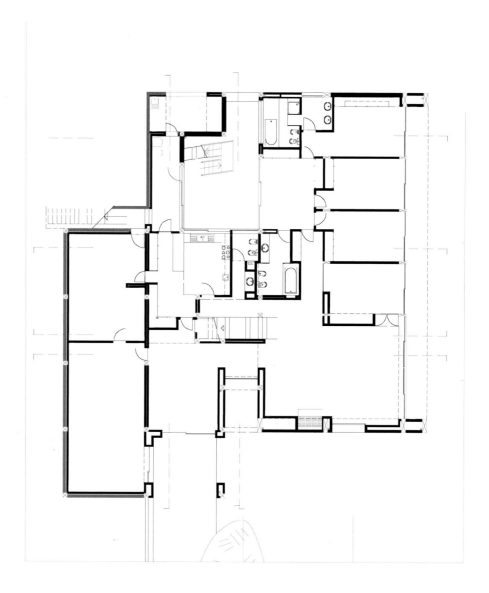

› Ground floor Rez-de-chaussée Erdgeschoss

Girona, Spain

Aiguablava

The Aiguablava House is the result of the renovation of an existing residence that, despite its prime location, was not oriented towards the sea, and thus lacked views of the water. For this reason, the objective of the project was to open the house on to the sea. The rear façade, which faces the cove, gained importance, as its windows were replaced with glass walls; the main façade, however, conserved its opaque walls to remain in harmony with its surroundings. The exterior was painted white, as were the stairs and handrails, to grant the air of a traditional Mediterranean house, while hanging gardens were laid on the gentle slope that leads from the entrance to the swimming pool. The interiors were rehabilitated to achieve a generously lit, spacious living room that enjoys views of the garden and the sea boynd. The furniture was chosen carefully: white pieces were combined with splashes of black to give a touch of colour.

La maison Aiguablava résulte de la restauration d'une habitation préexistante, qui, malgré sa situation privilégiée, n'étant pas orientée vers la mer manquait de vues. C'est pour cette raison que l'objectif de ce projet était d'ouvrir la maison sur la mer. La façade arrière, qui donne sur la calanque, a gagné de l'importance, car les fenêtres se sont transformées en murs de verre. Par contre, la façade principale a préservé ses murs opaques pour rester en harmonie avec les alentours. L'extérieur a été peint en blanc, comme les escaliers et les balustrades, à l'image de l'architecture méditerranéenne traditionnelle. La pente douce qui descend de l'entrée vers la piscine est parée de jardins en terrasse. Les intérieurs ont été transformés en un grand salon regardant sur le jardin et la mer, inondé de lumière naturelle qui se diffuse dans toute la maison. Le mobilier a été soigneusement choisi : blanc, émaillé de noir, il apporte une touche de couleur.

Das Haus Aiguablava entstand durch die Renovierung eines bereits existierenden Hauses, das zwar an einem wundervollen Ort stand, aber nicht zum Meer hin lag und so keinen Ausblick bot. Deshalb sollte das Haus zum Meer hin geöffnet werden. Die hintere Fassade, die zur Bucht liegt, gewann an Bedeutung, da aus den Fenstern Glaswände wurden. Die Hauptfassade hingegen behielt ihre undurchsichtigen Mauern, um die Harmonie mit der Umgebung zu bewahren. Das Haus wurde außen weiß gestrichen, ebenso die Treppen und Geländer, eine Anpassung an die traditionelle mediterrane Architektur. Der leichte Abhang vom Eingang zum Swimmingpool wurde für hängende Gärten genutzt. Innen wurde ein großes Wohnzimmer mit Blick auf den Garten und das Meer geschaffen, in das reichlich Tageslicht fällt, das das ganze Haus erhellt. Die Möbel wurden sorgfältig ausgewählt, weiß mit kleinen schwarzen Einschüben, die alles etwas farbiger wirken lassen.

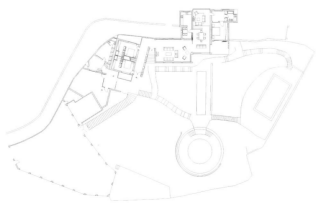

› Ground floor Rez-de-chaussée Erdgeschoss

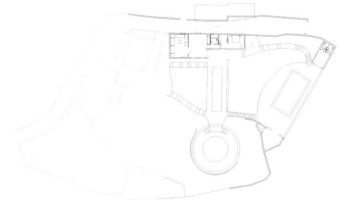

› Basement Sous-sol Kellergeschoss

The bedroom and the bathroom reflect the simple shapes and white décor that dominate the entire house.

La chambre à coucher et la salle de bains reflètent les formes simples et prônent un décor blanc qui domine tout l'ensemble.

Das Schlafzimmer und das Badezimmer weisen auch die einfachen Formen und die weiße Dekoration auf, die das gesamte Haus dominieren.

Cromer Residence
Résidence Cromer
Haus Cromer

Melbourne, Australia

This ensemble comprises a pair of two-story volumes joined by a structure that serves as the entrance to the home. The arrangement with respect to the terrain is different in each block: one is parallel to the site, while the other crosses it slightly. The second block is distinctive in that its lower level is set back considerably from a first floor resting on a series of beams, one of which extends beyond the structure. This upper floor presents a diaphanous interior with two levels, and contains the daytime areas: the kitchen and dining room are on one level and the living room on the other. The kitchen counter extends all the way into the living room and acts as a bar, which reinforces the connection between the two spaces. Both the forms and the range of materials used are reminiscent of the architecture of the Australian coast.

Cet ensemble est composé de deux volumes de deux étages unis par un bloc qui sert d'accès à l'habitation. La disposition sur le terrain n'est pas la même pour les deux volumes : l'un est parallèle au terrain, et l'autre est légèrement en biais. Ce dernier volume présente une particularité : l'étage inférieur est considérablement en retrait du rez-de-chaussée qui s'appuie sur des poutres, une d'entre elles dépassant de la structure. L'étage supérieur est doté d'un intérieur diaphane à deux niveaux et accueille les zones de jour : cuisine et salle à manger sur un niveau et salon sur l'autre. Le comptoir de la cuisine se prolonge jusque dans la salle à manger et sert de bar, ce qui sublime le lien entre les deux espaces. Les réminiscences de l'architecture australienne côtière se retrouvent tant dans les formes architecturales que dans l'éventail de matériaux utilisés.

Dieses Haus ist in zwei doppelstöckigen Blöcken angelegt, die durch einen Körper verbunden sind, in dem der Zugang liegt. Die beiden Blöcke sind in ihrer Anordnung auf dem Gelände unterschiedlich. Einer verläuft parallel zum Grundstück, während der andere es leicht durchquert. Der letzte Block hat ein ganz besonderes Kennzeichen; das untere Geschoss ist etwas vom ersten Stock zurückgesetzt, und der erste Stock steht auf Pfeilern, die über die Struktur hinausstehen. Dieses Obergeschoss hat transparente Räume auf zwei Ebenen, in denen die Bereiche für den Tag liegen, die Küche und das Esszimmer auf einer Ebene und das Wohnzimmer auf der anderen. Die Küchentheke reicht bis ins Wohnzimmer und dient als Bar, so dass beide Räume miteinander verbunden sind. Sowohl die architektonischen Formen als auch die vielfältigen verwendeten Materialien spielen auf die australische Küstenarchitektur an.

The massive cubes, the cantilevered upper stories and the materials are typical of Australian coastal architecture.

Les cubes massifs, les étages en encorbellement et les matériaux employés sont typiques de l'architecture côtière australienne.

Die massiven Würfel, die Stockwerke auf Vorsprüngen und die verwendeten Materialien sind typisch für die Architektur an der Küste Australiens.

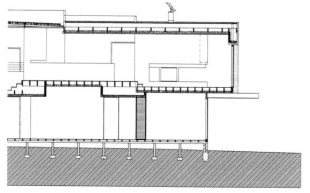

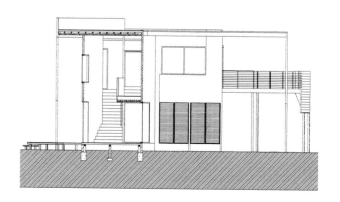

› Sections Sections Schnitte

The materials used in the interior include dark wood, hardwood floors and a plaster finish on the walls.

Les matériaux employés pour les intérieurs déclinent menuiseries sombres, sols en bois noble et finitions en plâtre sur les murs.

Die im Inneren verwendeten Materialien sind dunkle Rahmen, Böden aus edlem Holz und Gips an den Wänden.

House on Cascade Lake
Maison à côté du lac Cascade
Haus am See Cascade

Cascade Mountains, USA

The peacefulness and beauty of this area make it a perfect enclave for a getaway residence. The ensemble, which comprises two volumes, is adapted to its dramatically sloping site. The top floor of the three levels is rotated with respect to the lower two and crowned with a sloping roof ending in a cantilever. This floor contains the sitting room and dining room, visually separated by the kitchen. The two lower levels hold the bedrooms, which are distributed consecutively along the length of the façade, so that they all benefit from the spectacular views of the lake. The other volume, which connects the main part of the house to the ground, has two stories: the top floor icontains the entance to the house, as well as space for two cars, and the lower level is for services. At the owner's request, a double-height rock-climbing wall was built, which also serves to link two bedrooms.

La tranquillité et la beauté qui émanent de ce lieu en font une enclave idéale, métamorphosant cette résidence en havre de paix et de repos. L'ensemble s'adapte parfaitement à la forte inclinaison du terrain par le biais de ses volumes. L'un des trois niveaux dispose d'un étage supérieur en rotation sur les autres, coiffé d'une toiture inclinée qui s'achève en encorbellement. Cet étage dispose d'un salon et d'une salle à manger, séparés visuellement par la cuisine. Les deux niveaux restants accueillent les chambres à coucher, distribuées en enfilade le long du pourtour de la façade, profitant ainsi des vues spectaculaires sur le lac. L'autre volume, que le terrain relie au bloc principal, dispose de deux niveaux : le niveau supérieur comprend l'accès et une aire de stationnement de deux places, et l'inférieur est réservé aux services. Pour satisfaire la demande du propriétaire, un mur couvrant deux hauteurs est consacré à l'entraînement de l'escalade, solution qui sert de lien entre deux chambres.

Die Ruhe und Schönheit der Natur machen diesen Ort ideal für ein Ferienhaus. Das Haus passt sich an die starke Neigung an, indem es in zwei Teilen angelegt wurde. Ein Teil hat drei Stockwerke, das oberste ist über die anderen zwei gedreht und wird von einem Dach mit Vorsprung gekrönt. In diesem Stockwerk liegen das Wohn- und Esszimmer, die visuell durch die Küche getrennt werden. Auf den anderen beiden Ebenen liegen die Schlafzimmer, die sich hintereinander an der Fassade entlang erstrecken, so dass man von allen Zimmern einen wundervollen Blick auf den See hat. Der andere Gebäudeteil, der das Grundstück mit dem Hauptgebäude verbindet, hat zwei Stockwerke. Im oberen Stockwerk liegen der Eingang und ein Parkplatz für zwei Autos und im unteren Teil die Installationen und funktionellen Bereiche. Für den Hausherrn wurde eine steinerne Kletterwand doppelter Höhe angelegt, die zwei Räume miteinander verbindet.

The balcony reinforces the cantilever of the upper volume and also functions as an overlook, given its ideal location.

Le balcon fait fonction de galerie exaltant l'encorbellement du volume supérieur à l'instar d'un mirador, dû à sa situation privilégiée.

Der Balkon ist gleichzeitig eine Galerie, die den oberen Vorsprung stützt und als Aussichtspunkt dient.

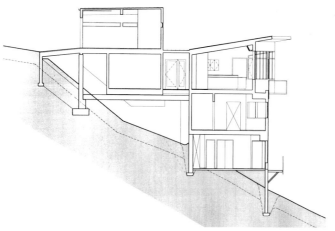

› Section Section Schnitt

› Situation plan Plan de situation Umgebungsplan

The cosy ambience of the interior was achieved through the use of light-toned wood throughout the house.

Les tons clairs de bois, omniprésents dans la maison, créent une ambiance intérieure accueillante.

Die klaren Holztöne im ganzen Haus schaffen eine einladende und warme Atmosphäre.

A number of surprising corners-such as a ship's cabin behind a doorway-conceal folding beds for extra guests if the need should arise.

Plusieurs coins insolites -derrière une porte, une cabine- cachent des lits pliants pour, le cas échéant, héberger un plus grand nombre de personnes.

In verschiedenen, ungewöhnlichen Ecken wie hinter einer Tür oder in einer Kabine befinden sich Klappbetten, um nötigenfalls viele Gäste unterbringen zu können.

Materials of a similar texture were used in the common areas, such as the kitchen, to enhance the spatial fluidity.

Dans les zones communes, à l'instar de la cuisine, l'emploi de matériaux de textures similaires accentue la fluidité spatiale.

In den gemeinsamen Bereichen wie in der Küche wurden Materialien mit ähnlicher Textur eingesetzt, um das Fließen des Raumes zu unterstreichen.

Wilson Residence
Résidence Wilson
Wilson Haus

Minnesota, USA

This rocky outcrop on the shores of Lake Vermillion is the site of a house designed to focus the attention on the views of the surrounding area. A series of parallel shapes flanks the main living room, which is the most important area in the house and the nucleus from which the remaining rooms are articulated. The master bedroom is oriented westward, while the remaining rooms face east. The formality of the two volumes is suddenly broken by a rocky outcrop from of the mountain and the systematic alteration in the fenestration. The living room faces a Victorian-style shutter that serves as a covered terrace and creates a transitional space between the interior of the house and its rugged surroundings. In contrast, the courtyard is designed on a smaller scale, to enclose and conceal the vistas of the lake before entering the house.

Cette enclave rocheuse sur les rives du lac Vermillion accueille une maison dont l'implantation tient compte avant tout des vues du paysage. Un premier agencement de formes parallèles constitue le grand salon, la zone la plus importante de l'habitation, autour de laquelle s'articule le reste des espaces. La chambre principale est orientée vers l'ouest, alors que les fonctions restantes sont orientées à l'opposé. La composition formelle des deux volumes est subitement rompue par l'avancée rocheuse de la montagne et le changement systématique du format des fenêtres. Le grand salon apparaît donc placé devant un store de type victorien sous forme de terrasse couverte et sert d'espace transitoire entre l'intérieur de la maison et l'extérieur champêtre. En contraste, le patio revêt une échelle plus petite, enfermant et masquant la vue du lac jusqu'à l'entrée dans la maison.

Auf diesem felsigen Gelände am Ufer des Vermillion Sees steht ein Haus, bei dessen Planung der Blick auf die Umgebung wichtigstes Element war. Das große Wohnzimmer wird von parallelen Formen begleitet. Es ist der wichtigste Raum des Hauses, von dem aus die restlichen Räume aufgeteilt werden. Das Hauptschlafzimmer liegt Richtung Westen, die übrigen Zimmer in die entgegengesetzte Richtung. Die Strenge der beiden Gebäudeteile wird plötzlich durch einen Felsen unterbrochen, auch die systematische Veränderung der Fenster lockert auf. Vor dem großen Wohnzimmerfenster wurde ein Rollladen im viktorianischen Stil angebracht, der auf eine bedeckte Terrasse zeigt, die als Verbindung zwischen dem ins Inneren des Hauses und der rauhen Umgebung dient. Der Hof ist klein, geschlossen und man hat von ihm aus keinen Blick auf den See.

The geography and nature of the site-a rocky area on the shores of a lake-evoke the landscape of the owners' native Sweden.

Les données géographiques et la situation de la parcelle, dans une zone rocheuse face au lac, évoquent le paysage suédois dont les propriétaires sont originaires.

Die Beschaffenheit und die Lage des Grundstücks in einem felsigen Gebiet vor dem See erinnern an die Landschaft Schwedens, einstige Heimat der Besitzer.

Despite regulations specifying a traditional design, modern details are present throughout the house in compositional language.

Malgré les composantes de type traditionnel imposées au projet, la composition du langage architectural est constamment émaillée de modernisme.

Obwohl bei dieser Planung zahlreiche traditionelle Gesichtspunkte berücksichtigt wurden, sind in die Gestaltung stets moderne Elemente aufgenommen worden.

› Situation plan   Plan de situation   Umgebungsplan

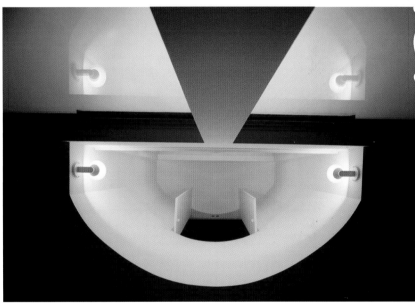

The white of the walls and ceilings is diluted by the light-coloured wood of the floor, banisters and the indoor pergola suspended above the salon.

Le blanc des murs et des plafonds se fond avec les détails du bois clair du sol, les balustrades et la galerie intérieure suspendue au-dessus du salon.

Das Weiß der Wände und Decken löst sich mit den Einzelheiten aus hellem Holz im Boden, den Geländern und der inneren Pergola, die über dem Wohnzimmer hängt, ab.

House and Art Gallery
Habitation et galerie d'art
Haus und Kunstgalerie

Massachusetts, USA

This project, by architects Kennedy and Violich, entailed the integration of an art gallery into a pre-existing home. The hybrid program of this intervention included a ballroom, an office to be equipped with the latest in telecommunications technology, an indoor pool, a contemporary modern art gallery, two outdoor courtyards and a sculpture garden. The building also had to hold this unusual program in one continuous space that would grant it enough wall space to hang the owner's vast art collection, which includes large-format works by such artists as Warhol, Oldenburg and Christo, as well as small paintings and engravings. To keep direct solar radiation from damaging the art, a skylight was designed that would reflect daylight and redirect it towards the gallery area. At night, this light source acts as a vacuum into which light from the fixtures on the ceiling refracts to create a peaceful and uniformly-lit setting.

Ce projet réalisé par les architectes Kennedy et Violich consiste à intégrer une galerie d'art dans une habitation préexistante. Ce programme hybride comprend également une salle de danse, un bureau équipé de systèmes de télécommunication de pointe, une piscine intérieure, une galerie d'art moderne et contemporain, deux patios extérieurs et un jardin de sculptures. Ce programme de construction inhabituel devait être réalisé dans un espace unique, fluide et doté d'une grande surface murale pour accrocher l'importante collection d'œuvres d'art du propriétaire : grands cadres à l'instar d'œuvres de Warhol, Oldenburg et Christo ainsi que des petites peintures et gravures. Une lucarne a été conçue pour renvoyer la lumière vers la zone d'exposition, afin d'éviter l'action néfaste des rayons de soleil sur les peintures. De nuit, ce puits de lumière agit comme un vide qui réfléchit la lumière des plafonniers créant une ambiance sereine et homogène.

In diesem Bauprojekt der Architekten Kennedy und Violich sollte eine Kunstgalerie in eine bereits existierende Wohnung integriert werden. Teil der mehrschichtigen Planung waren ein Tanzsaal, ein Büro mit modernster Telekommunikationsausstattung, ein Swimmingpool im Inneren, eine Galerie für moderne und zeitgenössische Kunst, zwei Höfe und ein Skulpturengarten. Diese ungewöhnlichen Räume sollten in einem einzigen, durchgehenden Raum mit genügend Wandfläche angelegt werden, um die umfassende Kunstsammlung des Besitzers auszustellen. Zu den großformatigen Bilden gehören Werke von Warhol, Oldenburg und Christo, sowie kleine Gemälde und Stiche. Damit das Sonnenlicht die Gemälde nicht beschädigt wurde ein Oberlicht geschaffen, das das Licht reflektiert und in den Ausstellungsbereich leitet. Nachts wirkt diese Lichtquelle wie ein Leerraum, der das Licht der Deckenlampen bricht und der eine strenge und einheitliche Atmosphäre schafft.

The pool starts in the centre of the gallery and extends to the edges of the house to end in a cantilever over the sculpture garden.

La piscine part du centre de la galerie et se prolonge aux confins de la construction pour se terminer en encorbellement au-dessus du jardin de sculptures.

Der Swimmingpool entspringt im Zentrum der Galerie und reicht bis zum Ende des Gebäudes, wo er auf einem Vorsprung über dem Skulpturengarten endet.

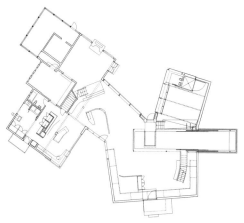

› First floor   Premier étage   Erstes Obergeschoss

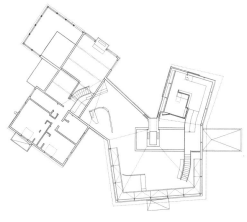

› Second floor   Deuxième étage   Zweites Obergeschoss

The pool is framed by a system of metal beams painted black that connect it to the gymnasium.

La piscine est entourée d'un système de menuiseries métalliques peintes en noir qui établissent le lien entre cette zone et le gymnase.

Der Swimmingpool wird von einem System aus schwarzen Metallrahmen umgeben, die es mit dem Fitnessraum verbindet.

Turba House
Maison Turba
Haus Turba

Novara, Italy

The aim of this project was to restore and join two existing structures without altering their traditional forms. Rather than modify the height or the distribution of spaces, the architects' criteria stemmed from traditional rural architecture. Thus, a double-height façade was built in front of the main building with openings cut in it to echo the openings of the original house. The space created between the old and new façades gave rise to a porch that acts as an entrance hall on the ground floor. The sequential layout of the bedrooms is adapted to the elongated distribution of the structure. The stairs that lead to the master bedroom, located on the first floor, designates the boundary between the day and night areas, which are also distinguished by the materials used in their finishing. Natural stone was used for the floor of the living room, while parquet was used in the bedrooms.

Ce projet a pour objectif de restaurer et réunir deux structures déjà existantes sans en altérer la typologie. Au lieu de modifier la hauteur ou la distribution des espaces, les architectes ont choisi une solution privilégiant les critères de la tradition architecturale rurale, pour aboutir à la construction d'une façade sur deux hauteurs devant l'édifice principal, dotée des mêmes ouvertures que l'originale. L'espace instauré entre l'ancienne et la nouvelle façade crée un atrium qui sert de vestibule d'accès au rez-de-chaussée. La disposition en enfilade des chambres résulte de la distribution en longueur de la structure. L'escalier qui dessert la chambre principale, située au premier étage, définit la séparation entre les zones de jour et de nuit, également différenciées par les matériaux employés. Le sol du salon est en pierre naturelle alors que les chambres sont revêtues de parquet.

Bei diesem Umbau sollten zwei bestehende Bauten miteinander verbunden werden, ohne dass dabei ihr Charakter verloren geht. Statt die Höhe oder die Verteilung der Räume zu ändern, haben die Architekten die Kriterien der traditionellen, ländlichen Architektur angewendet. So wurde eine Fassade doppelter Höhe vor dem Hauptgebäude errichtet, in der die gleichen Fenster wie am Originalgebäude geöffnet wurden. In dem Raum zwischen der alten und der neuen Fassade befindet sich eine Veranda, die gleichzeitig Eingangshalle zum Erdgeschoss ist. Aufgrund der länglichen Struktur der Gebäude sind die Zimmer hintereinander angeordnet. Die Treppe, die zum Hauptschlafzimmer im ersten Stock führt, dient als Unterteilung der Bereiche für Tag und Nacht, die auch durch die Materialien voneinander unterschieden werden. Die Fußböden im Wohnbereich sind mit Naturstein belegt, in den Schlafzimmern liegt Parkett.

The porch, suported by slender columns, leads to the inside of the house; depending on the time of day, it is a perfect spot to take shelter from the sun.

L'atrium, aux sveltes colonnes de soutien, mène à l'intérieur de l'habitation : à certaines heures du jour, c'est un espace idéal pour s'abriter du soleil.

Die Veranda wird von zwei schlanken Säulen gehalten und führt zum Inneren des Wohnhauses. Hier kann man zu bestimmten Tageszeiten den kühlen Schatten genießen.

The wooden beams are a recurring element throughout most of the house, running along the length of the ceiling, they represent an attempt to keep in touch with tradition.

Les poutres de bois, s'étirant le long du toit, sont l'élément commun à l'ensemble de l'habitation et la façon de faire revivre le passé traditionnel, idée de base du projet.

Ein gemeinsames Element in weiten Teilen des Hauses sind die Holzbalken an der Decke. Dieses Element erinnert an die Vergangenheit des Gebäudes.

The sitting room and dining room share a single space, while the kitchen is situated opposite them.

Le salon et la salle à manger partagent le même espace tandis que la cuisine est située de l'autre côté.

Das Wohn- und das Esszimmer befinden sich im gleichen Raum, während die Küche genau auf der anderen Seite liegt.

The bedrooms are all floored with parquet, which blends perfectly with the rustic style of the house.

Le parquet, le seul revêtement utilisé dans les pièces à vivre, se marie parfaitement au style rustique de l'ensemble.

In den Räumen wurde Parkett als einziger Bodenbelag benutzt. Es passt perfekt zum rustikalen Stil des Hauses.

The furniture has the additional function of lending a visual order to these spaces.

Les meubles ont une double fonction, car ils contribuent aussi à l'organisation visuelle de l'espace.

Die Möbel erfüllen eine doppelte Funktion, da sie den Raum visuell ordnen.

Spring Prairie Residence
Résidence Spring Prairie
Haus Spring Prairie

Wisconsin, USA

In this project, an old farmhouse was converted into a new residence by increasing its floor area through the addition of irregularly-shaped modules. The new house encompasses a number of bedrooms, bathrooms, a solarium, a dining room, shed, a small loft to enjoy the stunning views and a stable. The team of architects wanted the house, as a whole, to resemble an outcrop of rocks-for this reason, each piece of the house is designed in such a way as to direct the flow of movement and to echo the landscape. Garofalo Architects, the designers of this house, use highly specialized technology in the design of their projects; this allows them to achieve highly unusual shapes in the houses they build. The 'nerves' of the roof are made of three-ply plywood, and before being set into place they were waterproofed with a plastic coating; inside, some of these beams are partially exposed, and between them the ceiling was finished in polished plaster.

Une ancienne construction abritant autrefois une grange a été réhabilitée en habitation dont la superficie a été élargie par des modules de formes irrégulières. La maison dispose de plusieurs chambres à coucher, de salles de bains, de solarium, d'une salle à manger, d'un auvent, d'une petite tour pour admirer les belles vues et d'une étable. L'équipe d'architectes voulait que la maison, dans son ensemble, ressemble à un petit groupe de rochers. C'est pourquoi, chaque pièce est conçue pour diriger le mouvement et le paysage. Le bureau d'architecture, Garofalo Architects, utilise la technologie de pointe pour concevoir ses projets, parvenant ainsi à construire des habitations dotées de formes inhabituelles. Les nervures formées par le toit sont en bois contreplaqué, de trois couches, imperméabilisées par une membrane de plastique avant d'être placées à l'extérieur. A l'intérieur, certaines nervures sont partiellement apparentes, séparées par du plâtre poli entre chacune d'elles.

Ein ehemaliger Bauernhof wurde in ein Wohnhaus umgebaut, indem die Nutzfläche durch Module mit unregelmäßigen Formen vergrößert wurde. Das Haus besitzt mehrere Schlafzimmer, Bäder, ein Solarium, ein Esszimmer, einen Schuppen, einen kleinen Turm, von dem aus man den Ausblick genießen kann, und einen Stall. Das Architektenteam wollte ein Haus schaffen, das einer Felsengruppe gleicht. Aus diesem Grund wurde jedes Teil so entworfen, als ob es die Bewegung und die Landschaft leiten könnte. Garofalo Architects arbeitet mit hochspezialisierter Designtechnologie, mit deren Hilfe ungewöhnliche Formen bei der Konstruktion von Häusern geschaffen werden. Die „Rippen", die das Dach bilden, sind aus dreilagigem Sperrholz, das mit einer Plastikhaut wasserdicht überzogen wurde. Manche dieser „Rippen" sieht man im Inneren; zwischen ihnen wurde polierter Gips angebracht.

As the house was built by adding on small spaces, the aim was to achieve the effect of a small village in the middle of the prairie.

Cette habitation a été construite en ajoutant des petits espaces pour ressembler à un petit village au cœur de la prairie.

Indem man ein Haus mit kleinen, angefügten Räumen schuf, sollte die Wirkung eines Dorfes mitten auf einer Wiese entstehen.

The 'nerves' that make up the structure of the roof were manufactured based on a computerized model.

Les nervures formant la structure de la toiture ont été conçues par ordinateur.

Die „Rippen", die die Dachstruktur bilden, wurden auf der Grundlage eines Computerentwurfes angefertigt.

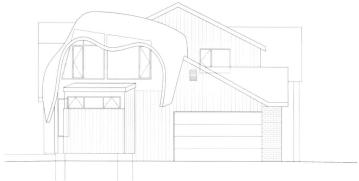

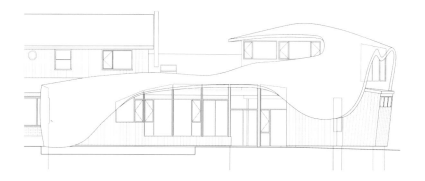

› Elevations Élévations Aufrisse

The simple mimicry of existing prototypes was discarded in favour of groundbreaking proposals, such as the bunk in this bedroom.

La structure existante n'a pas été imitée laissant place à des idées audacieuses, à l'instar du lit superposé de cette chambre à coucher.

Um die bereits existierenden Elemente nicht einfach nur nachzuahmen, wurden sehr auffällige Lösungen wie die Schlafkojen in diesem Schlafzimmer geschaffen.

Coppola Residence
Résidence Coppola
Haus Coppola

Pavia, Italy

This house rises above an irregular terrain, surrounded by a sea of vineyards. Its structure, which was entirely prefabricated, is supported by a cement foundation that plunges 50 feet into the ground. Structurally, it comprises two forms under a single roof. One is a one-story, double-height space that houses the living room, dining room and kitchen, while the other has two levels, which are divided into bedrooms, bathrooms, service areas and an attic. The considerable length of the façade and the openings cut into it are designed to take maximum advantage of the spectacular views that surround the house. The interior is a mixture of traditional materials with other, more contemporary ones, and the décor features pieces the owner brought back from visits to Indonesia, Nepal and Thailand.

Cette maison s'élève sur une enclave au relief accidenté, entourée d'immenses vignables. Sa structure, entièrement préfabriquée, est soutenue par des fondations fixées à 15 m de profondeur. Elle est constituée de deux volumes partageant le même toit : un rez-de-chaussée avec entresol qui abrite le salon, la salle à manger et la cuisine et un autre à deux étages accueillant les chambres, les salles de bains, les pièces de service et des combles dans la partie la plus haute. La façade tout en longueur et ses ouvertures sont dessinées pour permettre de profiter au maximum des vues spectaculaires qui entourent l'habitation. L'intérieur décline un mélange de matériaux traditionnels et contemporains, agrémenté d'objets décoratifs collectionnés au fil des voyages du propriétaire en Indonésie, au Népal et en Thaïlande.

Dieses Haus erhebt sich auf einem hügeligen, von großen Weinbergen umgebenen Grundstück. Die gesamte Fertighausstruktur steht auf einem Fundament, das 15 m unter der Erde befestigt ist. Die Struktur des Hauses wird von zwei Blöcken gebildet, die sich ein Dach teilen. Einer der Blöcke hat einziges Stockwerk doppelter Höhe, in dem sich das Wohnzimmer, das Esszimmer und die Küche befinden und der andere unterteilt sich zwei Ebenen, auf denen die Schlafzimmer, die Badezimmer, die funktionellen Räume und im obersten Bereich eine Mansarde liegen. Die Fassade ist ziemlich lang und die Fenster sind so gestaltet, dass man den wundervollen Blick auf die Umgebung wirklich genießen kann. Im Inneren werden traditionelle Materialien mit anderen zeitgenössischeren Materialien gemischt. Der Eigentümer hat sein Haus mit Gegenständen geschmückt, die er von seinen Reisen durch Indonesien, Nepal und Thailand mitbrachte.

The outside hearkens back to the traditional American house. Inside, the sliding doors both illuminate the house and conversely open it up to the garden.

L'extérieur rappelle les maisons traditionnelles américaines. A l'intérieur, les portes coulissantes contribuent à favoriser la luminosité et à tourner l'espace vers le jardin.

Das Haus erinnert von außen an traditionelle amerikanische Häuser. Schiebetüren lassen viel Licht nach innen fallen und beziehen den Garten mit in das Innere ein.

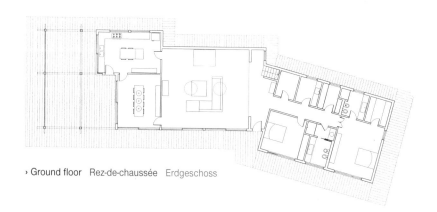

› Ground floor Rez-de-chaussée Erdgeschoss

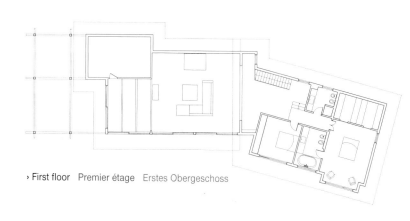

› First floor Premier étage Erstes Obergeschoss

Sutterlüty House
Maison Sutterlüty
Haus Sutterlüty

Vorarlberg, Austria

Nestled amidst the high mountains of the Alps, this light structure houses a single-family home. To the southeast, the site slopes down along an idyllic meadow. The volume of the house, a three-story rectangle crowned with a sloping pitched roof, is aligned in parallel to the slope of the terrain and the access road. Likewise, this east-west orientation allows the house to make the most of natural light and the vistas all around it. The entrance and the storage area are located on the northeast side and act as an insulating buffer for the rest of the house. The house opens its embrace to the southeast through a series of large windows, while the rest of the building is covered in delicate wooden slats. The kitchen and dining room are located on the middle floor, and the upper floor is given over to bedrooms.

Située au sein des hautes montagnes dans la chaîne des Alpes, cette construction légère s'élève et abrite une habitation unifamiliale. Vers le sud-est, le terrain présente une pente qui se transforme en prairie idyllique. Le volume, une pièce rectangulaire de trois étages couronnée par une toiture inclinée à deux pans, est parallèle à l'inclinaison de la pente et à la voie d'accès. A son tour, cette position sur l'axe est-ouest permet de profiter au maximum des vues et de la lumière solaire. L'accès et la zone d'entrepôt se trouvent sur la face nord-est et jouent le rôle de coussin thermique pour le reste de la maison. Vers le sud-est, la maison s'ouvre complètement grâce à de grandes baies vitrées, alors que le reste de l'édifice est couvert d'un fin lambris de bois. La cuisine et la salle à manger sont situées à l'étage intermédiaire, et les chambres à coucher sont installées à l'étage supérieur.

Zwischen den hohen Bergen der Alpen erhebt sich dieses leicht gebaute Einfamilienhaus. Im Südosten des Hauses liegt ein Hang mit einer idyllischen Wiese. Das dreistöckige Haus hat einen rechteckigen Grundriss und wird von einem Satteldach gekrönt, das parallel zur Neigung des Hangs und zum Zugangsweg verläuft. Durch die Ausrichtung von Ost nach West wird das Sonnenlicht maximal ausgenutzt und man hat einen wundervollen Blick. Der Zugang und die Lagerräume befinden sich auf der nordöstlichen Seite und dienen so zur Isolierung der anderen Räume. Im Südosten befinden sich große Fenster, während der Rest des Hauses mit feinen Holzlatten verkleidet ist. Im mittleren Geschoss liegen Küche und Esszimmer, im oberen die Schlafzimmer.

The ample, elongated terraces, which face southeast, are repeated on all the floors to create a continuous gallery.

Les vastes terrasses allongées, tournées vers le sud-est, se répètent à chaque étage créant ainsi une galerie continue.

Die weiten, langen Terrassen in Richtung Südosten sind in jedem Stockwerk zu finden. So entstand eine durchgehende Galerie.

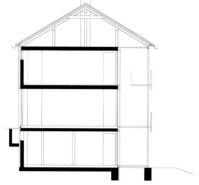

› Cross section Section transversale Querschnitt

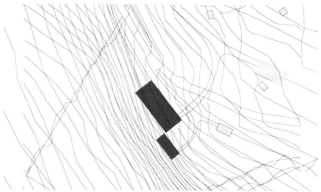

› Situation plan Plan de situation Umgebungsplan

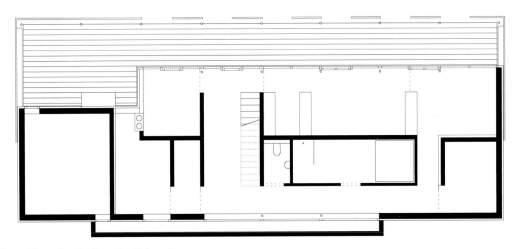

› Ground floor   Rez-de-chaussée   Erdgeschoss

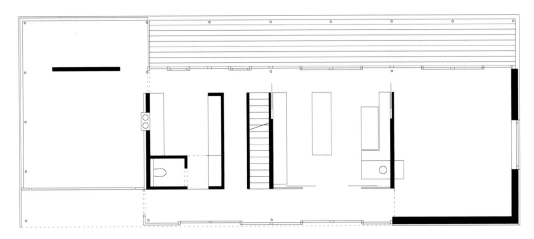

› First floor   Premier étage   Erstes Obergeschoss

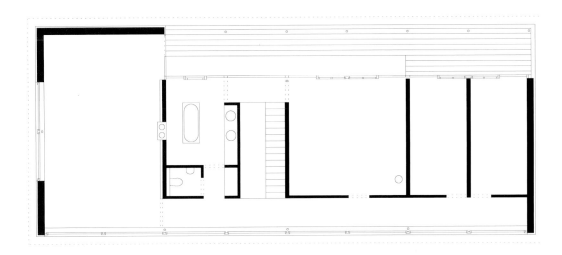

› Second floor   Deuxième étage   Zweites Obergeschoss

Adda Valley Residence
Résidence Adda Valley
Haus Adda Valley

Bergamo, Italy

This house, designed by architect Gino Guarnier overlooks the Alps, reflects the concept of the landscape as a purified expression of nature. The house thus serves as an observatory to draw the landscape inside and transform it into a decorative object for its owners to contemplate. Two levels divided into five functional areas organize the habitable space. The studio and dining room are located on the ground floor; while the upper level contains the lounge, kitchen, bedrooms and an independent guest room. The materials and finishes were chosen in an attempt to create a cosy atmosphere: the floors are clad with resin, the walls are painted white and the stairway is made of iroko wood. To round out this climate of well-being, a natural-stone hearth was built for the owners to enjoy on the coldest days of the year.

Cette habitation, située face aux Alpes, est l'œuvre de l'architecte Gino Guarnier : conçue à partir du paysage, elle est l'expression épurée des alentours. Cette maison, à l'instar d'un observatoire, fait entrer le paysage à l'intérieur et le transforme en élément de décor pour que ses habitants puissent le contempler. La surface habitable s'articule autour de deux niveaux subdivisés en cinq zones fonctionnelles. Le rez-de-chaussée accueille le studio et la salle à manger, le niveau supérieur, le salon, la cuisine, les chambres à coucher et une chambre d'amis indépendante. Les matériaux et finitions ont été choisis pour créer une ambiance accueillante : revêtement en résine pour le sol, murs blancs et bois d'iroko pour l'escalier. L'installation d'une cheminée en pierre naturelle, diffusant une douce et agréable sensation de chaleur les jours annuels de grand froid, parachève cette atmosphère de bien-être.

Innerhalb des architektonischen Konzeptes dieses, von dem Architekten Gino Guarnier entworfenen Hauses vor den Alpen ist die Landschaft ein bereinigter Ausdruck der Umgebung. Das Wohnhaus wurde als eine Art Observatorium angelegt, das die Landschaft nach innen trägt und in ein dekoratives Objekt verwandelt, das von den Bewohnern betrachtet werden kann. Zwei Ebenen sind in fünf funktionelle Bereiche unterteilt, die die bewohnbare Fläche ausmachen. Im Erdgeschoss befinden sich ein Atelier und ein Esszimmer, im Obergeschoss das Wohnzimmer, die Küche, die Schlafzimmer und ein unabhängiges Gästezimmer. Die Materialien und Oberflächen schaffen eine einladende Atmosphäre. Der Fußbodenbelag ist aus Kunstharz, die Wände sind weiß und die Treppe ist aus Iroko. Ebenso trägt ein Kamin aus Naturstein für die kälteren Tage im Jahr zur Gemütlichkeit bei.

The dining room is in a privileged location in the house, as it takes advantage of the natural light that filters in through the large windows.

La salle à manger occupe la place d'honneur dans cette maison, profitant de la lumière naturelle diffusée par les grandes baies vitrées.

Das Esszimmer befindet sich in einem besonders schönen Bereich des Hauses. Hier fällt das Tageslicht durch große Fenster ein.

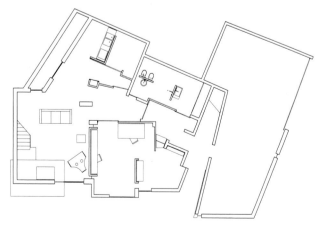

> Ground floor   Rez-de-chaussée   Erdgeschoss

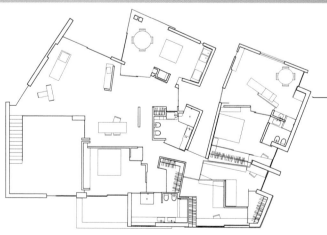

> First floor   Premier étage   Erstes Obergeschoss

The master bedroom, which opens onto a small terrace, has an adjacent bathroom with an almost invisible shower protected by a glass screen.

La pièce principale, ouverte sur une petite terrasse, dispose d'une salle de bains annexe avec une douche à peine visible, masquée par un paravent de verre.

Das Hauptschlafzimmer hat eine kleine Terrasse und ein anliegendes Bad mit Dusche, die durch eine kaum sichtbare Glaswand abgeschirmt wird.

Villa Novellino

Milan, Italy

The design of this home aimed to find a structure capable of both keeping out noise and blending into the surroundings. To achieve the first objective, the architect opted to employ a specific palette of materials in combination with a strategic layout. Thus, solid bearing elements and compact walls with carefully calculated openings were chosen for the main façade. To meet the second goal, the space that remained between the house and the street was turned into a garden and fitted with a pool. Inside, the ground floor is characterized by an approximately three-foot drop that delineates the distribution of activities: the dining room and the kitchen are located below, while the living room and master bedroom are on the higher level. The house has an additional two bedrooms on the second floor, each of which has its own terrace.

La conception de cette habitation vise à créer une structure permettant de s'isoler du bruit tout en se fondant à l'environnement. Le premier objectif a été atteint en choisissant de conjuguer une gamme de matériaux spécifiques à une stratégie de distribution de l'espace. A celà s'ajoute le choix d'éléments porteurs résistants et de murs compacts dotés d'ouvertures soigneusement étudiées sur la façade principale. Le second objectif a été atteint grâce à l'aménagement d'espace vert dans la partie restante entre l'habitation et la rue et à la construction d'une piscine. A l'intérieur, le rez-de-chaussée présente une dénivellation d'environ un mètre qui définit la distribution des activités : la salle à manger et la cuisine se trouvent dans la partie basse, alors que la zone du salon et la chambre principale sont installées au niveau supérieur. L'habitation comprend encore deux chambres situées au deuxième étage, chacune d'elles disposant de sa terrasse privée.

Ziel bei der Planung dieses Hauses war es, eine Struktur zu schaffen, die Lärm abschirmt und sich gleichzeitig in die Umgebung einfügt. Um den Lärm zu mindern, wurde eine Reihe von geeigneten Materialien strategisch verteilt eingesetzt. So wählte man solide, tragende Elemente und kompakte Mauern, und die Verteilung der Fenster in der Hauptfassade ist gut durchdacht. Um das Haus in die Umgebung einzufügen, wurde ein Garten mit einem Swimmingpool zwischen dem Haus und der Straße angelegt. Im Untergeschoss gibt es einen Höhenunterschied von ungefähr einem Meter, der die Aufteilung der Aktivitäten markiert. Das Esszimmer und die Küche befinden sich im niedrigeren Teil, während das Wohnzimmer und das Hauptschlafzimmer im oberen Teil liegen. Es gibt noch zwei weitere Zimmer im zweiten Stock, jedes davon hat eine eigene Terrasse.

Most of the windows were oriented towards the interior courtyard to minimize noise from the street.

La majorité des fenêtres est orientée vers le patio intérieur pour atténuer le bruit provenant de la rue.

Die meisten der Fenster liegen zum Innenhof, um den Lärm von der Straße zu veringern.

The brick walls insulate the house from noise and protect its owners' privacy.

Les murs de brique insonorisent l'intérieur et protègent l'espace privé des regards indiscrets.

Die Wände aus Ziegelstein dämpfen den Lärm und schützen vor indiskreten Blicken.

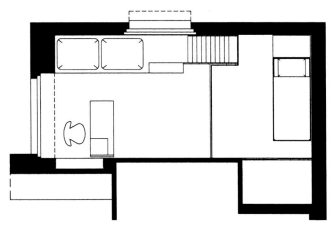

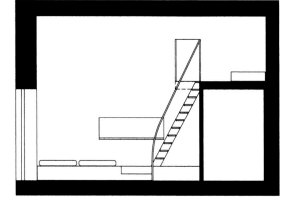

› Ground floor Rez-de-chaussée Erdgeschoss

› Section Section Schnitt

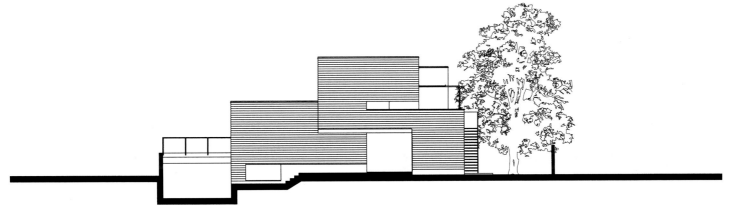

› Longitudinal section   Section longitudinale   Längsschnitt

House in Concepcion
Maison à Concepcion
Haus in Concepcion

Concepcion, Chile

This project arose out of a close collaboration with the client, an engineer who wished to live in a residential area far from the city. The site is situated near a beach, amidst a strange yet unique forest of pines, whose slender trunks branch out into a thick canopy some four metres from the ground. As both the architects and the client were enthusiastic about the visual poetry of this landscape, they worked together to preserve its essence. They opted to build three units of different dimensions that would combine to create a compact ensemble. Two of these structures-one made of wood and the other of concrete-are located at ground level, while the third, composed of metal and glass, is held up by metal supports and reaches up to the canopy of trees. Despite the variety of materials used in their construction, the three units blend in perfectly with the surrounding area.

Ce projet est né d'une étroite collaboration avec le client, un ingénieur dont l'intention était de vivre dans une zone résidentielle éloignée de la ville. Le terrain est situé près d'une plage, au cœur d'une dense forêt de pins aux caractéristiques particulières : des troncs fins aux couronnes épaisses qui naissent à quatre mètres de hauteur. Les architectes et le propriétaire, tombés mutuellement sous le charme de ce paysage poétique, ont travaillé ensemble pour préserver son essence. Ils décidèrent de construire trois unités de dimensions distinctes dont l'union engendre un ensemble compact. Deux de ces structures -une en bois et l'autre en béton- sont implantées au niveau du sol, alors que la troisième, alliant le métal et le verre, s'élève sur des pilotis de métal comme si elle voulait toucher la cime des arbres. Malgré la variété des matériaux utilisés dans la construction, les trois unités se fondent parfaitement à l'environnement.

Dieses Haus entstand in enger Zusammenarbeit mit dem Kunden, ein Ingenieur, der in einem Wohngebiet weit von der Stadt entfernt zu leben wünschte. Das Grundstück befindet sich in der Nähe des Strandes inmitten eines dichten Waldes voller eigentümlicher Pinien mit feinen Stämmen, gekrönt von dichten Wipfeln, die ungefähr auf vier Meter Höhe beginnen. Die visuelle Poesie dieser Landschaft begeisterte die Architekten und den Eigentümer, so dass sie zusammen arbeiteten, um deren Essenz zu wahren. Es wurden drei Einheiten mit verschiedenen Abmessungen konstruiert, die so kombiniert sind, dass sie eine kompakte Gruppe schaffen. Zwei dieser Strukturen, eine aus Holz und eine aus Beton, befinden sich auf Bodenhöhe, während die Dritte aus Metall und Glas auf Metallstützen steht und sich bis zu den Baumkronen erhebt. Obwohl sehr verschiedene Materialien verwendet wurden, verschmelzen die drei Einheiten perfekt mit ihrer Umgebung.

The simple forms of the house, its compact dimensions and the intelligent use of materials allow the volume to adapt perfectly to the exuberant coppice of pines that surrounds it.

Les formes simples de la maison, ses dimensions compactes et l'emploi judicieux des matériaux permettent au volume de s'adapter à l'exubérance du bois de pins environnant.

Die einfachen Formen des Hauses und der intelligente Einsatz der Materialien machten es möglich, dass sich das Gebäude in den üppigen Pinienwald einfügt.

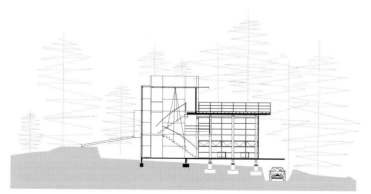

› Section Section Schnitt

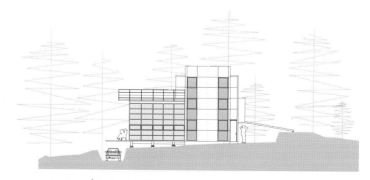

› Elevation Élévation Aufriss

The single-height kitchen area contrasts with the double-height ceilings of the living room, located on the same level.

La zone de la cuisine, d'une seule hauteur, contraste avec la hauteur double du salon, situé sur le même niveau.

Der Küchenbereich einfacher Höhe steht im Gegensatz zu dem Wohnzimmer mit doppelt hohen Decken, das sich auf der gleichen Etage befindet.

Villa 1

Lanaken, Belgium

This house was designed in response to a strict series of requirements set by the clients: the structure was to blend into its surroundings yet clearly indicate the layout of its interior. The fence and exterior walls were designed in line with the pattern set by the neighbouring houses; as a result, the house is in perfect harmony with its surroundings. Nevertheless, the beds and plants in the two gardens flanking the house act guarantee of its inhabitants' privacy. In the interior, the spaces are distributed sequentially and progressively open to the exterior as an extension of the garden. In keeping with the desire to create an integrated architectural composition, materials were chosen to combine easily with the overall look. Thus, an ochre-coloured limestone, wood and grayish zinc were chosen for the roof and the structure-a palette that effortlessly pleases the eye.

La conception de cette habitation répond à des critères stricts fixés par les clients : l'intégration de la structure à l'environnement et une distribution claire et visible des différentes sphères de vie. La clôture et les murs extérieurs ont été conçus sur le modèle des maisons limitrophes, permettant l'intégration harmonieuse de l'ensemble à l'environnement. Les parterres et la végétation des deux patios de la maison ont la fonction de protéger l'intimité de ses habitants. A l'intérieur, la distribution joue avec une enfilade d'espaces qui s'ouvrent progressivement vers l'extérieur comme s'ils prolongeaient le jardin. Dans un souci de créer une composition architecturale harmonieuse, les matériaux sélectionnés sont faciles à combiner pour créer une image d'ensemble : le choix d'une pierre calcaire ocre, de bois et de zinc grisâtre pour le toit et la structure, décline une palette de tons qui crée un extérieur très paisible.

Die Kunden hatten für dieses Haus ihre Anforderungen genau definiert. Die Struktur sollte sich in die Umgebung einfügen, die Verteilung der verschiedenen Bereiche sollte klar und deutlich sein. Die Umzäunung und die Außenmauern wurden ähnlich der angrenzenden Häuser gestaltet, um das Haus harmonisch in die Nachbarschaft einzubinden. Die Gartenanlagen und die Vegetation der beiden Höfe an den Seiten des Hauses schützen die Intimsphäre der Bewohner. Im Inneren wird mit einer Abfolge von Räumen gespielt, die sich langsam nach draußen öffnen, eine Art Verlängerung des Gartens. Um eine integrierte architektonische Gestaltung umzusetzen, wurden Materialien ausgewählt, die sich leicht mit dem Aussehen der ganzen Gebäudegruppe kombinieren lassen. Die Struktur und das Dach sind aus ockerfarbenem Kalkstein, Holz und gräulichem Zink. Diese Zusammenstellung lässt das Haus sehr ruhig wirken.

The elevations and sections testify to the complexity of the juxtaposition of the different volumes making up the structure.

Les tracés et les sections mettent en évidence la complexité de la juxtaposition des volumes structuraux.

Die Aufrisse und die Schnitte zeigen, wie komplex die Nebeneinanderstellung der strukturellen Blöcke ist.

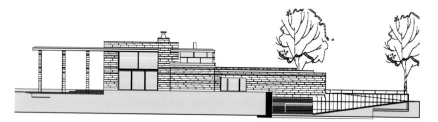

› Cross section   Section transversale   Querschnitt

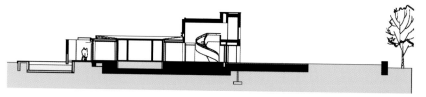

The two stories of the house are connected by a peculiar stairway-it is a sinuously curving wooden structure that rises to the second level.

Les deux étages de l'habitation sont reliés par un escalier insolite : une structure de bois qui s'élève en torsades jusqu'au palier du second étage.

Die beiden Stockwerke des Hauses werden durch eine eigentümliche Treppe verbunden, eine Holzstruktur, die sich in den zweiten Stock windet.

As one of the premises of the design was to preserve the relationship with the exterior, extensive windows were designed to run the length of the structure.

D'énormes baies vitrées parcourent la structure, en réponse à l'une des idées directrices de préserver le lien avec l'extérieur.

Eine der Voraussetzungen bei der Planung war es, die Beziehung mit der Umgebung aufrecht zu erhalten. Deshalb wurden große Fensterflächen in die Struktur eingesetzt.

Inside, different materials intermingle in a play of textures and colors that yields a comfortable and balanced interior.

A l'intérieur, les matériaux s'entremêlent dans un jeu de textures et de couleurs pour créer un intérieur confortable et harmonieux.

Im Inneren mischen sich die Materialien in einem Spiel mit Texturen und Farben, was die Räume komfortabel und ausgeglichen wirken lässt.

Spine Residence
Résidence Spine
Haus Spine

Colonia, Germany

This house is divided into two independent wings by an ellipsoid volume on top of a series of tall, slender columns-this volume serves as the spine of the house and runs from north to south. In addition to separating the two wings, this element-the defining feature of the design-extends the house outdoors, beyond the limits of the structure. Likewise, on the inside, it houses an ample, usable space that contains the living room and a loft. The complex extends out over the street elevation and narrows toward the garden, which means that the south façade offers extensive views from the bedroom on the first floor and the studios on the lower level. The roof is flat and is plated in zinc. As the house was designed to be a refuge from its owners' exhausting workdays, it includes such leisure spaces as a squash court, a pool and an art gallery.

Cette maison est partagée en deux ailes indépendantes par un volume ellipsoïde formant une arrête, orientée nord-sud, qui repose sur des piliers fins et élancés. Cet élément, caractéristique principale du projet, n'a pas uniquement une fonction de séparation, mais également d'extension de la maison vers l'extérieur : en dépassant les limites structurelles de la maison, il en accroît la superficie habitable, hébergeant à l'intérieur un salon et un mirador. Le complexe s'étend au-dessus de la rue et s'étire jusque vers le jardin, permettant aux chambres à coucher du rez-de-chaussée ou au studio de l'étage inférieur de se lover derrière les vues de la façade sud. La couverture plane est revêtue de zinc. Le projet a été conçu comme un refuge où les propriétaires pourraient s'isoler après leurs journées de travail épuisantes. Ces derniers ont donc tenu à l'installation d'espaces ludiques, à l'instar d'une piste de squash, d'une piscine et d'une zone réservée à une galerie d'art.

Dieses Haus wird von einem Ellipsoid in zwei unabhängige Flügel unterteilt. Dieses Ellipsoid formt einen Körper, der sich auf hohe, feine Säulen stützt und von Norden nach Süden verläuft. Dieses Element, der auffallendste Teil der Konstruktion, dient nicht nur der Trennung, sondern es verlängert das Haus auch nach draußen, da es die strukturellen Begrenzungen überwindet. Es vergrößert die Wohnfläche, da sich in seinem Inneren ein Wohnzimmer und eine Aussichtsterrasse befinden. An der Straße ist der Komplex breiter, zum Garten hin wird er schmäler, so dass man von der Südfassade aus die Schlafzimmer im ersten Stock oder die Ateliers im daruntergelegenen Stockwerk sehen kann. Das flache Dach ist mit Zink verkleidet. Das Haus sollte ein Zufluchtsort nach den anstrengenden Arbeitstagen der Besitzer sein. Deshalb ließen sie sich einen Squashplatz, einen Swimmingpool und eine Kunstgalerie anlegen.

The stairway that connects the lower level with the loft aligns with the double doors that open to the garden.

L'escalier connectant le rez-de-chaussée au mirador est en alignement avec les portes doubles d'accès au jardin.

Die Treppe verbindet das Erdgeschoss mit der Aussichtsterrasse. Ihr Verlauf orientiert sich an den doppelten Türen, durch die man den Garten betritt.

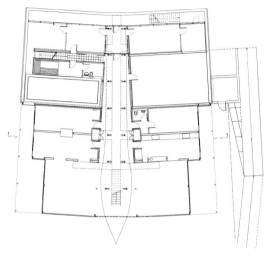

› Ground floor   Rez-de-chaussée   Erdgeschoss

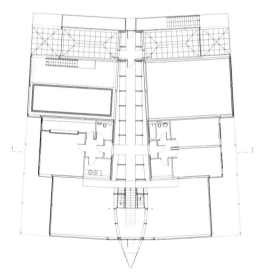

› First floor   Premier étage   Erstes Obergeschoss

236

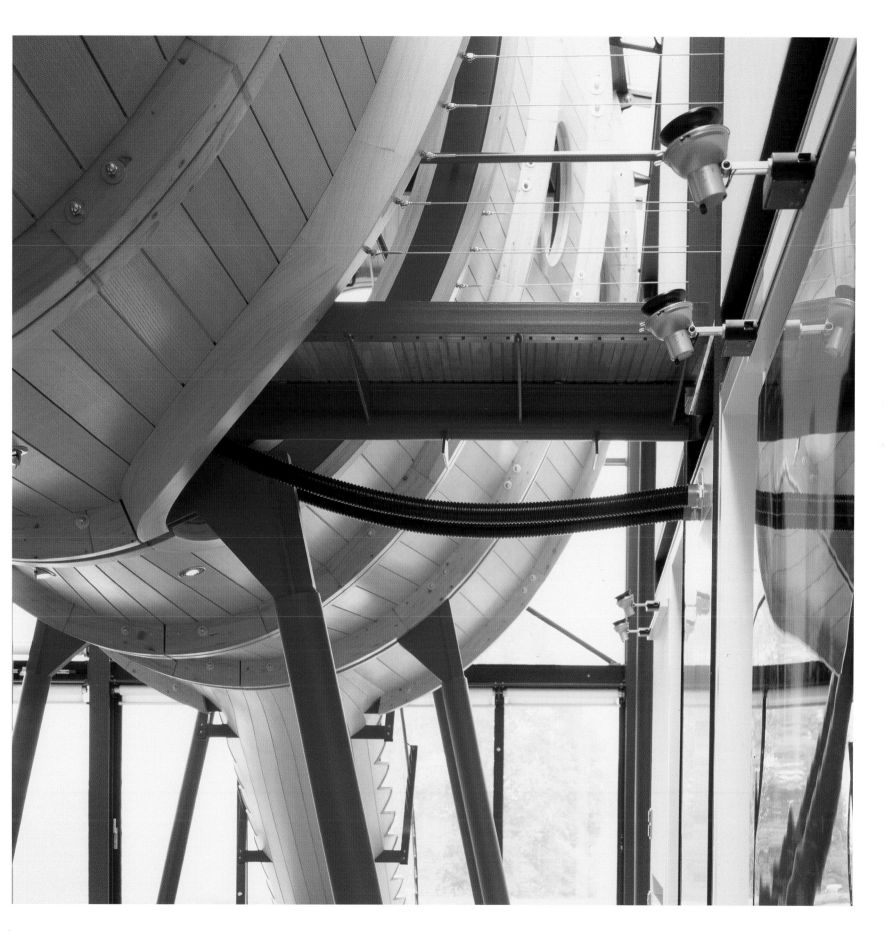

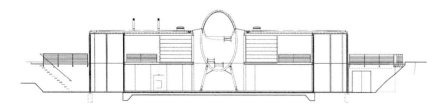

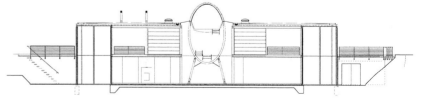

› Cross sections Sections transversales Querschnitte

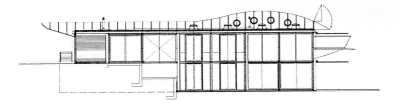
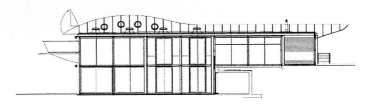

› Longitudinal sections   Sections longitudinales   Längsschnitte

The spine, handcrafted in wood by local carpenters, is divided into eight sections.

L'arrête, construite en bois travaillé artisanalement par les charpentiers de la région, est divisée en huit sections.

Der Holzkörper, der von Hand von den örtlichen Schreinern angefertigt wurde, ist in acht Bereiche unterteilt.

Clement Residence
Résidence Clement
Clement Residenz

California, USA

Bearing in mind the warm climate of California's coast, the architects from the firm commissioned to design this house decided to build a compact volume with a reduced number of small openings, so that the house would have greater thermal inertia. Despite this design, however, the house establishes a close relationship with the exterior. Rather than exhibiting a conventional distribution on separate floors, the house is a succession of different levels that are created by spaces of different heights. The main room is centered around a low, multifunctional piece that encompasses a hearth, television, storage area and shelving, which separates the dining room from the lounge without creating a visual boundary. The materials used are wood and reinforced concrete, and the palette of tones in ochre evokes the arid landscape of the area surrounding the house.

Pour s'adapter à la chaleur de la côte californienne, les architectes de l'entreprise chargés du projet de construction de cette résidence ont décidé d'élever un volume compact doté d'un nombre réduit de petites ouvertures, afin que l'inertie thermique provienne de la structure elle-même. Malgré cette conception, la maison est en étroite relation avec l'extérieur. A l'intérieur, loin de suivre une distribution conventionnelle stratifiée en étages, le projet opte pour une série de niveaux différents créant des espaces de hauteur variable. La zone de vie principale est dominée par un élément polyvalent qui accueille la cheminée, la télévision, l'espace de rangement et quelques étagères. Ce meuble bas sépare la salle à manger du salon sans marquer de délimitation visuelle. Les matériaux employés sont le bois et le béton armé et la palette des tons ocre évoque le paysage aride qui entoure l'habitation.

Um das Haus an das warme Klima der kalifornischen Küste anzupassen, entschieden sich die Architekten für eine kompakte Form mit wenigen, kleinen Öffnungen, so dass die Struktur selbst die thermische Trägheit fördert. Trotz dieses Gestaltungsmerkmals hat das Haus ein enges Verhältnis zur Umgebung. Innen sind die Räume nicht konventionell auf Stockwerke verteilt, sondern viele verschiedene Ebenen folgen aufeinander, so dass Räume verschiedener Höhen entstehen. Das Hauptzimmer wird von einem multifunktionellen Element beherrscht, in dem sich der Kamin, der Fernseher, Lagerraum und ein paar Regale befinden. Dieses niedrige Möbelstück trennt das Esszimmer vom Wohnzimmer, ohne eine visuelle Barriere darzustellen. Die verwendeten Materialien sind Holz und Stahlbeton. Die verschiedenen Ockertöne empfinden die karge Landschaft der Region nach, die die Wohnung umgibt.

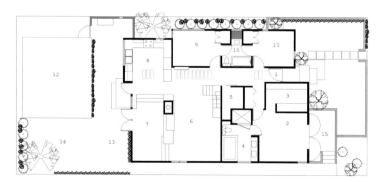

› Ground floor Rez-de-chaussée Erdgeschoss

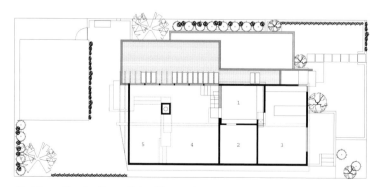

› First floor Premier étage Erstes Obergeschoss

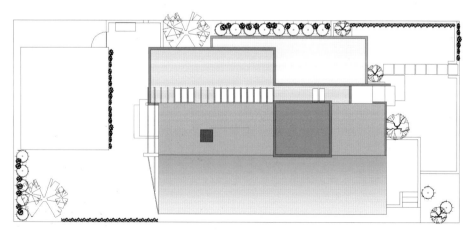

› Top floor Niveau couvert Dachgeschoss

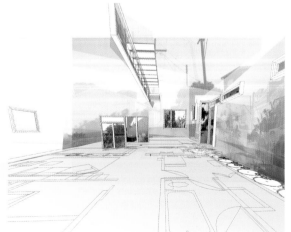

› Perspective Perspective Perspektivzeichnung

C House
Maison C
Haus C

Tokyo, Japan

The C House is a small yet complex building, which fulfils two different urban programs: a studio and a public café, both owned by the same person. This combination of two programs, which is more than a simple juxtaposition of functions, is a reflection of contemporary urban life, where the limits between the private and public spheres are blurred. The C House is an architectural manifestation of this reality, and can be understood as a prototype of a city in a single building. The transparent spaces of the café, located on the ground floor and the rooftop terrace, literally envelop the opaque volume that contains the private area of the house. The two parts of the program have independent exits on to the street, yet they are internally connected, accentuating the fluidity between the two.

La maison C est un édifice, petit et complexe à la fois, abritant deux programmes urbains distincts : un studio et un café de commerce, appartenant tous deux à la même personne. L'association des deux programmes, plus qu'une juxtaposition de fonctions, est le reflet de la vie urbaine contemporaine où se profilent les limites entre la sphère privée et publique. La maison C reflète la matérialisation architecturale de cette réalité et représente en quelque sorte un prototype urbain en un seul édifice. Les salles transparentes du café, installées au rez-de-chaussée et la terrasse, entourent littéralement le volume opaque qui abrite les fonctions de la partie privée. Les deux parties du programme architectural disposent d'accès indépendants depuis la rue, mais communiquent aussi entre elles par l'intérieur, sublimant la fluidité spatiale des deux zones.

Das Haus C ist ein kleines, aber gleichzeitig komplexes Gebäude, das zwei verschiedenen Funktionen dient. In dem Gebäude sind ein Atelier und ein Café untergebracht, die beide der gleichen Person gehören. Die beiden Programme wurden so verbunden, das nicht einfach nur die Funktionen nebeneinander gestellt wurden, sondern das zeitgenössische Stadtleben widergespiegelt wird, wo die Grenzen zwischen Privatsphäre und Öffentlichkeit allmählich in Erscheinung treten. Das Haus - C ist also die architektonische Materialisation dieser Wirklichkeit und wird so zu einer Art urbaner Prototyp in einem einzigen Gebäude. Die transparenten Räume des Cafés im Erdgeschoss und das Flachdach umgeben die undurchsichtigen Gebäudeteile, in denen die Privaträume des Hauses liegen. Für beide Bereiche gibt es unabhängige Zugänge von der Straße aus, aber gleichzeitig sind sie miteinander verbunden, was den fließenden Übergang zwischen beiden Zonen noch unterstreicht.

The transparent structures, situated on the ground floor and the terrace, delimit the café area and envelop the opaque central structure, which is the café owner's home.

Les structures transparentes, situées au rez-de-chaussée et la terrasse, délimitent la zone du café et enveloppent la structure centrale opaque, résidence du propriétaire.

Die transparenten Strukturen des Erdgeschosses und der Terrasse grenzen das Café ab und umgeben die zentrale, undurchsichtige Struktur, die Wohnung des Eigentümers.

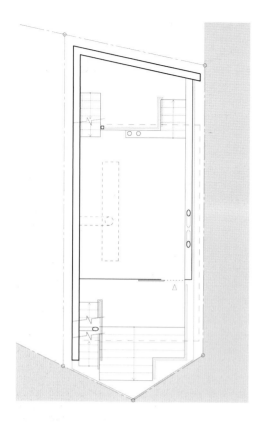

› Ground floor Rez-de-chaussée Erdgeschoss

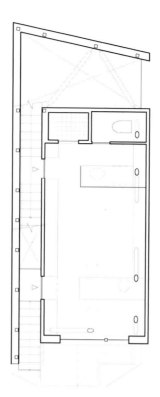

› First floor Premier étage Erstes Obergeschoss

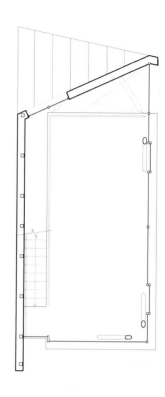

› Second floor Deuxième étage Zweites Obergeschoss

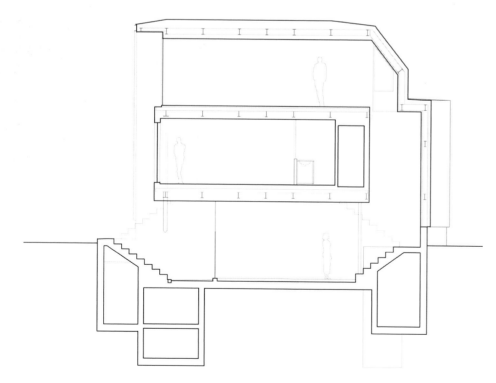

› Longitudinal section Section longitudinale Längsschnitt

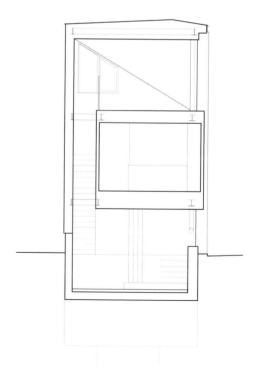

› Cross section Section transversale Querschnitt

As though it were it a lookout tower, the transparent, windowed structure of the café allows customers to capture the essence of the surroundings.

A l'instar d'un mirador, la structure transparente et vitrée de la cafétéria permet de capter l'essence de l'environnement.

So als ob es sich um einen Aussichtspunkt handelte erfasst die transparente, verglaste Struktur des Cafés die Essenz der Umgebung.

To achieve a greater degree of connectivity between the café and the residential area, a stairway was designed to connect the two.

Un escalier a été conçu pour mieux relier la cafétéria à la zone de résidence, unissant ainsi les deux univers.

Um eine stärkere Verbindung zwischen Café und der Privatwohnung zu erreichen, wurde ein Treppe entworfen, die beide Bereiche verbindet.

Smarthouse

Rotterdam, the Netherlands

This house forms part of a series of prototypes, dubbed smarthouses, that offer many advantages over traditional houses. Although they can vary in length, they are all built around steel-beam skeletons. The vertical and horizontal enclosures are fixed to the metal skeleton and the interior is divided by means of mobile partitions to create versatile and functional spaces. It is also possible to modify the various parts of the house and reorganize its levels. Likewise, two units can be joined to form one single apartment, which achieves double-height spaces and a greater openness; this is the case of the Smarthouse Modelwoning. Furthermore, the design permits the placement of windows anywhere on the façade to take maximum advantage of the available natural light. All these parameters can be decided during the design phase, and they do not affect the budget or the construction time, which usually amounts to three months.

Cette habitation fait partie d'un ensemble de prototypes surnommés « smarthouses » qui offrent de multiples avantages. Ce sont des habitations construites à partir d'un squelette constitué de poutres d'acier à longueur variable. Les parements verticaux et horizontaux sont fixés au squelette métallique et les divisions intérieures sont des cloisons amovibles générant des espaces modulables et fonctionnels. Il est parfaitement possible de modifier les sphères de vie de l'habitation et d'en réorganiser les niveaux. Pour cela, deux appartements peuvent être réunis en un seul pour obtenir des espaces sur deux hauteurs, plus ouverts : c'est le cas du Modelwoning. En outre, la conception permet de disposer les fenêtres à n'importe quel endroit de la façade pour tirer parti au maximum de la quantité de lumière naturelle. Tous ces paramètres peuvent être prévus dans la phase de conception et n'affectent en rien ni le devis ni le temps de réalisation de l'œuvre, fixé à environ trois mois.

Dieses Haus gehört zu einer Reine von Prototypen, die „Smarthouses" genannt werden und viele Vorteile bieten. Die Häuser sind über ein Skelett aus Stahlträgern konstruiert, deren Länge variieren kann. Die vertikalen und horizontalen Wände und Decken werden an diesem Metallskelett befestigt und die inneren Raumteiler sind mobil, so dass vielseitige und funktionelle Räume entstehen. Man kann auch die Wohnbereiche und die Ebenen verändern. Dazu können zwei Wohnungen als eine benutzt werden, so dass man einen offeneren Raum doppelter Höhe erhält, wie dies bei Modelwoning der Fall ist. Außerdem ist es möglich, die Fenster an jeglichem Punkt der Fassade anzubringen, um so viel Tageslicht wie möglich in die Räume zu lassen. Das kann alles in der Gestaltungsphase entschieden werden, wobei die Kosten und die Bauzeit sich nicht erhöhen. Die normale Bauzeit beträgt ungefähr drei Monate.

The floors of these prototypes seek out the maximum efficiency: they optimize surface area and avoid inactive trajectories or unused corners.

Les plans de ces prototypes visent un maximum d'efficacité : optimiser la surface au sol et éviter les trajectoires inactives ou les recoins inutiles.

Der Grundriss dieser Prototypen ist so effizient wie möglich gestaltet, die Nutzflächen werden optimiert und nicht genutzte Wege oder Ecken werden vermieden.

› Plans Plans Grundrisse

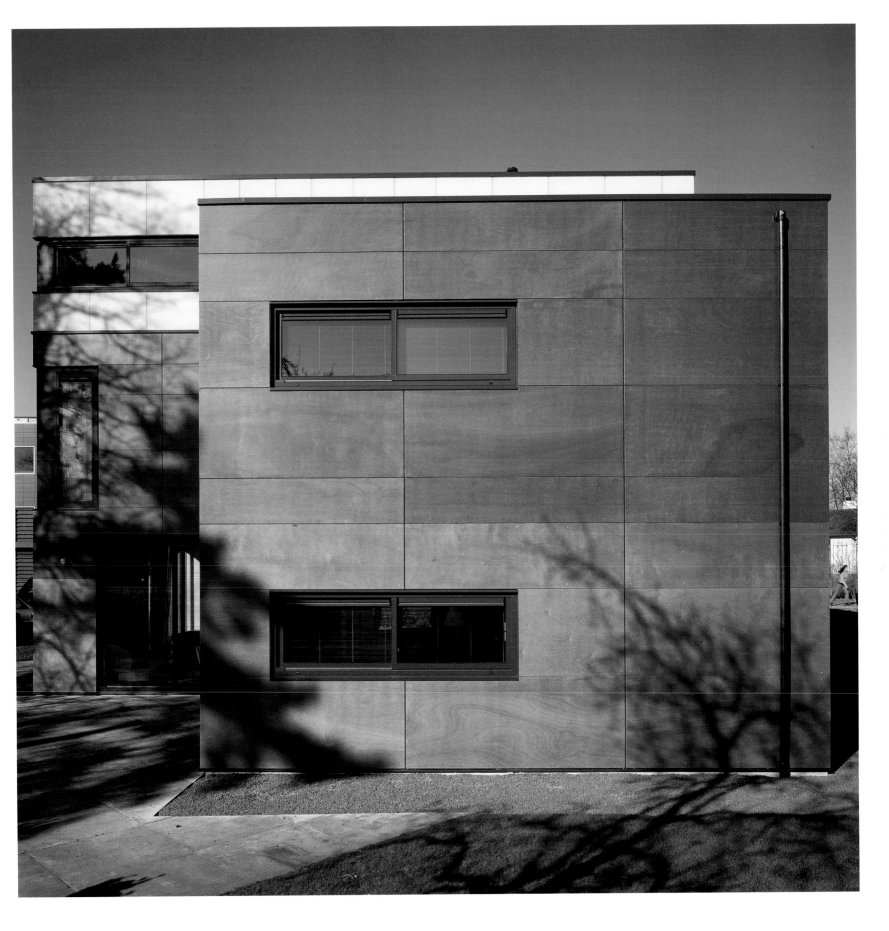

The interiors represent a commitment to versatility, as they offer the possibility of generating multifunctional spaces that adapt to personal requirements.

Les intérieurs répondent au pari de la polyvalence en offrant la possibilité de créer des espaces modulables adaptés aux besoins de chaque client.

Es wurde vor allem auf Vielseitigkeit Wert gelegt. Es können multifunktionelle Räume geschaffen werden, die sich an die Anforderungen des jeweiligen Kunden anpassen lassen.

Lingg Residence
Résidence Lingg
Haus Lingg

Bregenz, Austria

The Lingg Residence is set on a hill overlooking Lake Constance. To the northeast, the house cuts into the ground to keep out the cold and to increase its thermal inertia. The concrete ground floor, which functions as a skirting board, contains the entrance, garage and mechanical rooms. The marquee created by the second floor, which extends nearly 6.6 feet out over the entrance, creates a comfortable intermediate space in which to welcome or see off visitors. Inside, the stairs are positioned against one of the perimeter walls and thus do not interrupt any of the domestic activities. On the top floor, this compartmentalisation disappears and the living room, kitchen and dining room occupy a single space that opens on to a terrace covered by the elongated roof.

La résidence Lingg est située sur une colline dans la banlieue de la ville et jouit de vues privilégiées sur le lac de Constance. Au nord-est, l'édifice, est inséré dans le terrain pour se protéger des températures les plus basses et augmenter ainsi l'inertie thermique de l'habitation. Le rez-de-chaussée en béton constitue le socle de l'habitation et accueille l'entrée, le garage et les pièces réservées aux installations. La marquise, créée par l'avancée de deux mètres du deuxième étage au-dessus de l'accès, offre un espace intermédiaire pratique et agréable, abrité pour accueillir ou dire au revoir aux amis. A l'intérieur, les escaliers sont installés juste à côté des murs qui entourent la maison et ne gênent en rien les activités domestiques. Le dernier étage est dépourvu de cloisonnement et le salon, la cuisine et la salle à manger occupent un seul espace tourné vers la terrasse couverte grâce à l'extension du toit.

Das Haus Lingg befindet sich auf einem Hügel außerhalb der Stadt, von dem aus man einen wundervollen Blick auf den Bodensee hat. Im Nordosten ist das Gebäude in den Boden eingefügt, um es vor der Kälte zu schützen und die thermische Trägheit zu erhöhen. Das aus Beton gebaute Erdgeschoss bildet den Sockel des Hauses. Hier befinden sich der Eingang, die Garage und der Heizungsraum. Der zweite Stock ragt fast zwei Meter über den Eingang hinaus und bildet so einen geschützten Platz, an dem man komfortabel Besucher empfangen oder verabschieden kann. Die Treppen liegen direkt an den Außenwänden des Hauses und unterbrechen so die Räume nicht. Im obersten Stock gibt es keine Zwischenmauern, so dass das Wohnzimmer, die Küche und das Esszimmer in einem einzigen Raum liegen, an den sich eine Terrasse anschließt, die von dem verlängerten Dach des Hauses bedeckt wird.

Only the south-facing stretch of the garden was paved; it is marked by reinforced concrete load-bearing walls.

Une terrasse occupe uniquement le tronçon de jardin orienté vers le sud où s'élèvent des murs de soutien en béton armé.

Nur der südliche Teil des Gartens wurde zur Terrasse. Hier wurden Umfassungsmauern aus Stahlbeton errichtet.

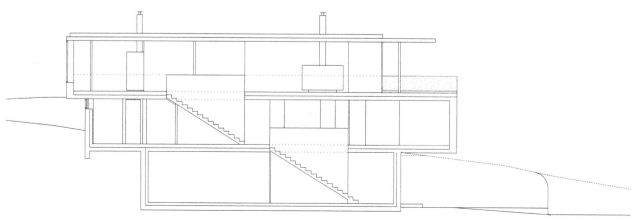

› Section Section Schnitt

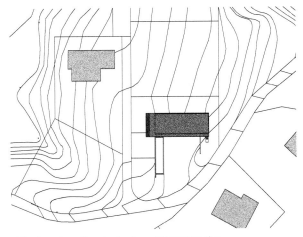

› Situation plan Plan de situation Umgebungsplan

All the bedrooms are located on the first floor: while the children's bedroom has direct access to the garden, the master bedroom enjoys views of the lake.

Le premier niveau accueille toutes les chambres à coucher, celles des enfants ont un accès direct au jardin et de leur chambre, les parents ont la vue sur le lac.

Im ersten Stock liegen alle Schlafzimmer. Von den Kinderzimmern aus gelangt man direkt in den Garten und vom Zimmer der Eltern aus blickt man auf den See.

In the lounge, the table divides the dining room and the relaxation area without visually interrupting the space or interfering with the views of the surroundings.

Au salon, seule la table le sépare de la salle à manger, l'espace dépourvu de cloisonnement, reste fluide et les vues sur les environs ne sont pas fractionnées.

Im Wohnzimmer bildet ein Tisch die Trennung zum Esszimmer, ohne dabei visuell den Raum oder die Aussicht zu unterbrechen.

The shifting floors created intermediate spaces in which the house's owners could enjoy the outdoors without suffering from inclement weather.

Le décalage de niveaux crée des espaces intermédiaires qui permettent aux usagers de la maison de profiter de l'extérieur, à l'abri des intempéries.

Durch die Abstufung der Stockwerke werden Zwischenräume geschaffen, durch die die Bewohner die Natur genießen können, ohne dem schlechten Wetter ausgesetzt zu sein.

Las Encinas Residence
Résidence Las Encinas
Residenz Las Encinas

Madrid, Spain

This house is located in a residential neighborhood, on a large site that guarantees the owners' privacy. The house itself was conceived as a geode-a solid, closed shell of granite that would contrast with large glass windows-in reference to the geodes that are commonly found in this rocky area. The house rises two stories above the ground and also has a basement, which contains the garage, a sunken courtyard and a vertical hall that leads to the upper levels. The main entrance, on the ground floor, is located in the courtyard of an outdoor parking area delineated by a recess carved out of the volume, which forms a low porch. The living room and services are located on the ground floor, which is a spectacular double-height space. The upper level is reserved for bedrooms.

Cette habitation se trouve dans un quartier résidentiel, sur un terrain aux dimensions généreuses assurant l'intimité des propriétaires. Le volume est conçu à l'instar d'une géode, un corps de granit, massif et fermé, contrastant avec le verre des grandes baies vitrées, analogue à la substance qui recouvre les grottes rocheuses. L'habitation s'articule autour de deux étages surplombant la pente et un sous-sol, abritant le garage, un patio sous-terrain et le vestibule vertical qui conduit aux étages supérieurs. L'accès principal au rez-de-chaussée est situé dans le patio du stationnement extérieur délimité par un espace en retrait, creusé dans le volume, formant une arcade basse. Le rez-de-chaussée accueille le salon et la zone de services et possède un espace sur deux hauteurs très spectaculaire. L'étage supérieur est réservé aux chambres à coucher.

Dieses Haus liegt in einem Wohnviertel auf einem großen Grundstück, das die Intimsphäre der Bewohner schützt. Das Gebäude ist in Art einer Geode angelegt, der Körper ist aus Granit, massiv und geschlossen, und steht im Gegensatz zu den großen Fenstern, die den Substanzen ähneln, die solche Felsenöffnungen zu bedecken pflegen. Das Haus hat zwei Stockwerke auf einem Gefälle und ein Kellergeschoss, in dem sich die Garage, ein in den Boden eingelassener Hof und eine vertikale Eingangshalle befinden, die in die oberen Stockwerke führt. Der Haupteingang im Erdgeschoss liegt im Hof des Parkplatzes außen und ist zurückgesetzt, wie eine Ausgrabung an einem Gebäude oder eine niedrige Vorhalle. Im Erdgeschoss liegen das Wohnzimmer und die funktionellen Räume. Außerdem gibt es einen beeindruckenden Raum doppelter Höhe. Im Obergeschoss befinden sich die Schlafzimmer.

The exterior of is a deconstruction of cubes that allows the observer to imagine the layout of the interior.

La structure extérieure s'apparente à des sortes de containers cubiques qui permettent d'imaginer la disposition des pièces à vivre à l'intérieur.

Die äußere Struktur wirkt wie eine Art würfelförmiger Behälter. Man kann sich die Anordnung der Räume im Inneren vorstellen.

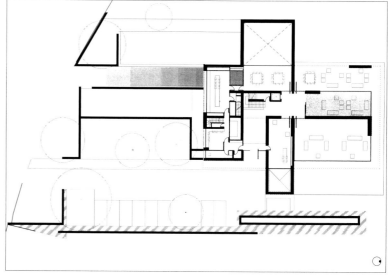

› Ground floor   Rez-de-chaussée   Erdgeschoss

› First floor   Premier étage   Erstes Obergeschoss

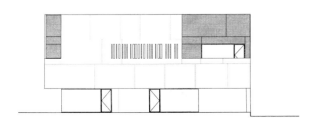

› Elevation Élévation Aufriss

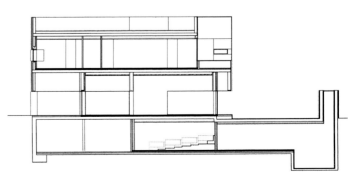

› Section Section Schnitt

The furniture defines the two areas of the ground floor-salon and dining room-the latter of which contains two rectangular dining tables.

La disposition des meubles définit l'atmosphère des deux pièces du rez-de-chaussée, le salon et la salle à manger, cette dernière disposant de deux tables rectangulaires pour les repas.

Das Erdgeschoss wird durch zwei rechteckige Tische in zwei Bereiche unterteilt, die Eingangshalle und das Esszimmer.

The spaces in this single-family home appear completely integrated thanks to the innovative and experimental way it uses materials.

Les espaces de cette habitation unifamiliale semblent complètement intégrés grâce aux solutions innovatrices et expérimentales réalisées à partir des matériaux.

Die Räume dieses Einfamilienhauses wurden durch die innovative und experimentelle Verwendung der Materialien perfekt integriert.

Residence in Hyogo
Résidence à Hyogo
Haus in Hyogo

Hyogo, Japan

The main intention of this design was to imitate the diversity of the region by means of a variety of spaces that would stimulate the senses. On entering the house, the visitor perceives it as a bridge over an unexplored terrain dominated by vegetation, a deep valley and a river. The living room is suspended in the air and opens on to a balcony that connects to the upper terrace by means of a spiral staircase. The lower level is reserved for the private areas of the house, where the bathroom is separated from the bedroom by a glass partition, which allows it to be flooded with morning light. The materials used, such as exposed concrete and metal, act as connecting elements between the various levels and also create an image that contrasts with the surrounding natural environment. Nature is present in every room, however thanks to the constant presence of glass.

Le projet avait pour critère essentiel d'imiter la diversité offerte par la zone par le biais d'une série d'espaces divers stimulant la perception. Dès l'entrée, le visiteur perçoit la maison comme un pont au-dessus d'un terrain vierge où la végétation, la vallée profonde et le fleuve sont omniprésents. Le salon est un lieu de séjour suspendu au-dessus du vide, ouvert sur un balcon qui communique avec la terrasse supérieure grâce à un escalier en spirale. Le niveau inférieur est réservé aux zones privées où la salle de bains est séparée de la chambre à coucher par un paravent de verre transparent, solution permettant à la lumière matinale d'inonder toute la salle. Les matériaux utilisés, à l'instar du béton brut et du métal, sont des éléments qui servent de lien entre les différents niveaux générant en même temps une image qui contraste avec le milieu naturel, même si le paysage est présent dans les moindres recoins grâce à l'omniprésence du verre.

Hauptziel bei diesem Haus war es, die Unterschiedlichkeit der Umgebung durch verschiedene Räume, die die Wahrnehmung anregen, zu imitieren. Vom Eingang aus wirkt das Haus wie eine Brücke über ein unerforschtes Gelände, wo es Vegetation, ein tiefes Tal und einen Fluss gibt. Das Wohnzimmer ist ein Raum, der im Leeren aufgehängt ist und einen Balkon hat, der mit der oberen Terrasse durch eine Wendeltreppe verbunden ist. Im unteren Stockwerk befinden sich die privaten Räume. Das Bad wird durch eine durchsichtige Glaswand vom Schlafzimmer getrennt, so dass der ganze Raum von der Morgensonne erhellt wird. Die benutzten Materialien wie unverputzter Beton und Metall dienen als Verbindungselement zwischen den verschiedenen Ebenen und schaffen gleichzeitig ein Bild, das mit der umgebenden Natur kontrastiert, obwohl die Landschaft aufgrund der zahlreichen Verglasungen stets präsent ist.

The succession of open and closed spaces, as well as their variety and arrangement, creates a labyrinth-like atmosphere that invites visitors to explore the house.

L'enfilade d'espaces ouverts et fermés, leur variété et disposition, créent un effet de labyrinthe qui incite à l'exploration de l'objet architectural.

Durch die Aufeinanderfolge von offenen und geschlossenen Räumen, ihre Vielseitigkeit und Anordnung entsteht eine labyrinthische Wirkung, die zum Erforschen des Hauses einlädt.

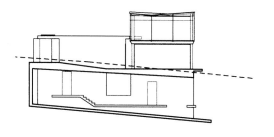

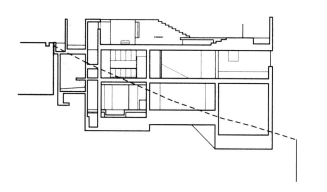

› Sections Sections Schnitte

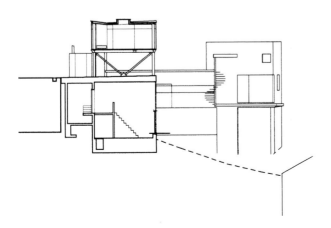

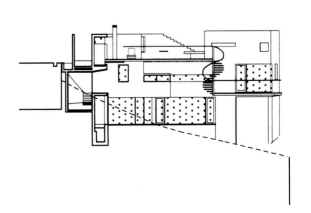

Double L
Deux L
Doppeltes L

Yokohama, Japan

Despite being located on a hill, this single-family home in a suburb of Tokyo is in a dense urban area. The design thus reconsiders the local conditions and creates a sequence of interrelated activities that relate back to the exterior. The overall L-shaped composition gives rise to an inner world in which the terraces and spaces oriented towards the resulting courtyard relate to one another-this design resulted in a great diversity of environments and numerous ways of taking advantage of every room in the house. The extension of the interiors on to the terraces is accentuated by following the same criteria for their finishes and materials. The result is an inner landscape that relates to the overall context of the neighbourhood. The austere façade facing the street is closed to the outside and engages in a dialogue with the surroundings.

Cette maison unifamiliale, située dans un quartier de Tokyo, a été conçue sur un site à fort caractère urbain, malgré sa situation dans les collines. Il fallut donc repenser la conception en fonction des conditions locales et créer une série d'activités reliées entre elles et avec l'extérieur. La forme en L de la composition générale permet de concevoir un univers intérieur où les différentes terrasses et espaces orientés vers le patio découlant de ce plan sont reliés entre eux. Cette conception engendre une grande diversité de situations et de nombreuses façons de tirer parti de chaque pièce à vivre de la maison. L'extension des intérieurs vers les terrasses s'accentue selon le même critère de finitions et de matériaux. Cela donne un paysage intérieur en relation avec le contexte général du quartier. Depuis la rue, la façade fermée et austère entre en dialogue avec les constructions environnantes.

Dieses Einfamilienhaus befindet sich in der Nähe von Tokio und steht auf einem Grundstück mit städtischem Charakter, obwohl es auf einem Hügel liegt. Diese durch das Grundstück vorgegebenen Bedingungen beeinflussten die Planung in der Weise, dass man versuchte, eine Reihe von miteinander und nach außen verbundenen Elementen zu schaffen. Durch die Anlage einer L-Form entstand eine innere Welt, in der verschiedene Terrassen und Räume, die zum Hof liegen, miteinander verbunden sind, so dass viele verschiedene Situationen und räumliche Möglichkeiten in dem Haus entstanden. Durch die Oberflächen und Materialien wurde die Lage der Räume zu den Terrassen hin noch unterstrichen. So entstand eine Landschaft, die mit dem allgemeinen Kontext des Viertels in Beziehung steht. Von der Straße aus wirkt die Fassade geschlossen und nüchtern, jedoch gut in die bebaute Umgebung integriert.

This double-height house is structured around a staircase that connects the various floors.

L'habitation, sur deux hauteurs, s'articule autour d'un escalier qui relie les différents étages.

Das Wohnhaus doppelter Höhe hat eine Treppe im Zentrum, die die verschiedenen Stockwerke miteinander verbindet.

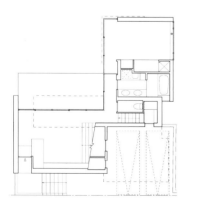
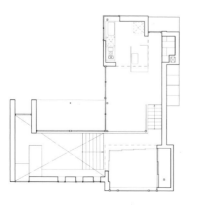
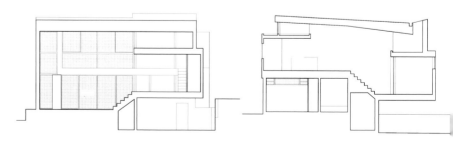

› **Ground floor** Rez-de-chaussée Erdgeschoss   › **First floor** Premier étage Erstes Obergeschoss   › **Sections** Sections Schnitte

Cliff Residence
Résidence Cliff
Residenz Cliff

Cape Town, South Africa

This house is situated on a pronounced, 45° slope on an elongated and narrow site. The program aimed to preserve the existing vegetation for reasons of privacy, as well as to take full advantage of the views. Due to the physical reality of the site, the house was designed as a narrow building organized along an orthogonal screen parallel to the contours of the land, so as to minimize excavation. This Cartesian composition, which is both transparent and light, rests on a solid base set back from the main volume. The entrance to the house on the middle floor, which leads to the living room-dominated by a large fireplace-followed by the kitchen and dining room. The stairway adjacent to the door leads to the lower level, which contains the bedrooms, as well as up to the top floor, which houses a study and terraces that offer a spectacular view of the nearby mountains.

Cette maison se décroche grâce à une forte pente de 45° degrés sur un terrain allongé et très étroit. La conception devait préserver l'écran végétal naturel pour des raisons d'intimité tout en tirant profit au maximum des vues existantes. Compte tenu des conditions physiques du terrain, l'habitation est un édifice étroit, organisé comme un réticule orthogonal parallèle au pourtour réduisant ainsi l'importance de l'excavation. Cette composition cartésienne, transparente et légère repose sur une base massive, en retrait du volume principal. L'accès à l'habitation se fait par l'étage intermédiaire qui s'ouvre sur le salon - dominé par une grande cheminée - la cuisine et la salle à manger. L'escalier contigu à l'entrée dessert le niveau inférieur, abritant les chambres, et l'étage supérieur, occupé par un studio et des terrasses avec de splendides vues panoramiques sur les montagnes environnantes.

Dieses Haus auf einem langen und sehr schmalen Grundstück hängt von einem Hang mit 45° Neigung herab. Die existierende Vegetation sollte erhalten bleiben, um vor Blicken zu schützen, gleichzeitig sollte man aber auch einen schönen Ausblick haben. Aufgrund der Grundstücksform wurde ein schmales Gebäude geschaffen, das wie ein rechtwinkliges Netz parallel zur Umgebung verläuft. So waren wenig Aushubarbeiten notwendig. Diese kartesianische, transparente und leichte Komposition ruht auf einer massiven Basis, die vom Hauptgebäude zurückgesetzt ist. Der Eingang befindet sich auf der mittleren Ebene. Daran anschließend liegen das Wohnzimmer mit seinem großen Kamin, die Küche und das Speisezimmer. Die Treppe am Eingang führt in das darunterliegende Geschoss mit den Schlafzimmern und in das höhere Geschoss mit dem Atelier und den Terrassen, von denen man einen wundervollen Panoramablick auf die Berge hat.

The elongated cube that makes up the house is interrupted and enriched by various elements that intervene at different points along its length.

Le cube aux proportions rectangulaires qui structure la maison est brisé et enrichi de nombreux éléments qui se succèdent au fil du paysage intérieur

Das Rechteck, das das Haus bildet, wird unterbrochen und im Inneren durch verschiedene Elemente bereichert.

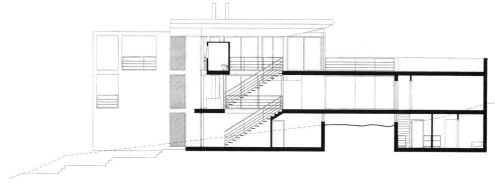

› Sections Sections Schnitte

Tea Gardens Residence
Résidence Tea Gardens
Tea Gardens Haus

New South Wales, Australia

The Tea Gardens Residence is set on a lot filled with trees and shrubs. Conceptually, the project consists of a series of walls that intersect with a prism resting on the ground. The walls running from north to south were painted blue, and the east-to-west walls were painted gray. The larger rooms, such as the living room, kitchen and dining room, enjoy ceilings of a generous height, while those in the bedrooms are much lower. The bathrooms, which are narrow and have high ceilings, direct attention outward. The floor plan of the house is brusquely interrupted by a stairway that makes a visual connection between the north-facing area on the upper floor and the summer terrace, which faces south. The windows are fitted with shades that strategically block out the summer sun. Likewise, the communal areas enjoy good ventilation in the form of soft breezes that grant respite from the heat.

La résidence Tea Gardens est située sur un terrain rempli d'arbres et d'arbustes. Sur le plan conceptuel, l'œuvre présente une série de murs qui se croisent avec un prisme installé sur le terrain. Les murs orientés nord-sud sont peints en bleu et les murs est-ouest sont gris. Les pièces à vivre les plus grandes, à l'instar du salon, de la cuisine ou de la salle à manger sont très hautes, les chambres étant plus basses. Les salles de bains, hautes et étroites, forcent le regard de l'usager vers l'extérieur. Le plan de l'habitation est brusquement interrompu par un escalier qui fait le lien visuel avec la zone de l'étage supérieur, donnant au nord et la terrasse d'été, orientée vers le sud. De l'autre côté, les fenêtres sont équipées d'écrans installés pour faire obstacle au soleil d'été. En outre, les zones communes disposent d'une excellente ventilation qui crée de douces brises pour atténuer la chaleur.

Das Tea Gardens Haus befindet sich auf einem Grundstück voller Bäume und Büsche. Das Gebäudekonzept beruht auf einer Reihe von Mauern, die sich mit einem Prisma schneiden, das auf das Grundstück gelegt wurde. Die Mauern nach Norden und Süden wurden blau gestrichen, die nach Osten und Westen grau. Die größeren Räume wie das Wohnzimmer, die Küche und das Speisezimmer sind sehr hoch, die Schlafzimmer niedriger. Die hohen, engen Bäder zwingen den Blick des Benutzers nach draußen. Das Erdgeschoss des Hauses wird brüsk von einer Treppe unterbrochen, die eine visuelle Verbindung zwischen dem in Richtung Norden liegenden Obergeschoss und der Sommerterrasse nach Süden schafft. Die Fenster sind mit Abschirmungen ausgestattet, die die Sommersonne nicht durchlassen. In den Gemeinschaftsräumen herrscht eine gute Lüftung, um ein Anstauen von Hitze zu vermeiden.

The house is divided into two levels: the semi-basement houses the garage, the water tank and a store room; the domestic rooms are located on the upper floor.

L'habitation s'articule sur deux niveaux : le demi-sous-sol accueille le garage, le réservoir d'eau et une réserve alimentaire. La partie domestique est située à l'étage supérieur.

Das Haus besteht aus zwei Ebenen, im Erdgeschoss befinden sich die Garage, Wassertank und ein Lagerraum, während die Wohnräume im Obergeschoss liegen.

One of the objectives was to design a house that would grow old without decaying, to thus be able to contemplate how time and weather would beautify its walls.

Un des objectifs était de concevoir un édifice qui vieillisse sans se détériorer, permettant de voir combien l'âge et les conditions météorologiques embellissent ses murs.

Es sollte ein Gebäude entstehen, das altert, ohne dass sich dabei sein Zustand verschlechtert. Zeit und Wetter sollten die Mauern versschönern.

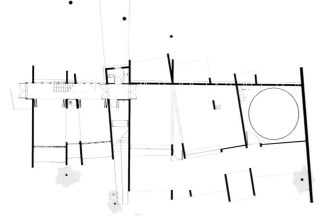

› Ground floor   Rez-de-chaussée   Erdgeschoss

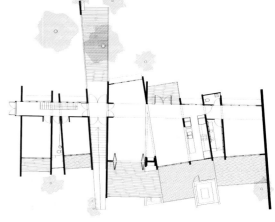

› First floor   Premier étage   Erstes Obergeschoss

› Cross section Section transversale Querschnitt

Between the dining room and the living room, a double passageway was created to allow the two spaces to be connected yet remain independent.

Entre la salle à manger et le salon, il existe une circulation à double sens qui permet de faire communiquer les deux espaces tout en leur assurant une certaine indépendance.

Zwischen dem Esszimmer und dem Wohnzimmer wurde ein doppelter Durchgang geschaffen, der beide Bereiche verbindet, aber auch voneinander unabhängig macht.

The design process was influenced by a profound awareness of the environment, which led to the creation of spaces that waste as little energy as possible.

La conception a été fortement influencée par une profonde conscience écologique, produisant des espaces avec une très faible perte d'énergie.

Bei der Planung konnte man auf gute ökologische Kenntnisse zurückgreifen, so dass Räume entstanden, in denen kaum Energie verloren geht.

House in High Bridge
Habitation à High Bridge
Haus in High Bridge

High Bridge, USA

This site is covered in a dense coppice of beeches, oaks and maples and drops 120 feet from one end to the other. The house that was built atop it adapts to these contours and its design is an abstraction of the existing topography. The design process was focused on creating a house that would be compact, flexible and easily accessed. The domestic program was defined in detail by the client, who was only to live there for half of the week. Thus, it was designed to have three bedrooms-two of which would be highly flexible in terms of size and use-as well as two bathrooms and a toilet. The dining room, living room and kitchen were considered to be extensions of a landscape that would enter into the domestic domain. The client also required a library, an office and a two-car garage. Various materials were used in the interior: ceramic tiles, varnished wood and polished stone.

Ce terrain, couvert d'un grand nombre de hêtres, chênes et érables, présente une dénivellation de 36 mètres d'un bout à l'autre. Il abrite une construction adaptée à l'environnement. Sur le plan architectural, c'est une abstraction de la topographie existante. Tous les efforts convergent pour créer une habitation à la fois modulable et facilement accessible. L'organisation du programme domestique a été définie en détails par la cliente qui n'occupe les lieux que la moitié de la semaine. Il y a donc trois chambres - d'eux d'entre elles devant être modulables sur le plan taille et usage - deux salles de bains et un cabinet de toilettes. La salle à manger, le salon et la cuisine sont perçues comme des extensions du paysage pénétrant le domaine familial. Il fallait aussi une bibliothèque, un bureau et un garage pour deux voitures. La diversité des matériaux définit l'intérieur : carreaux de céramique, bois vernis et pierre polie.

Inmitten eines dichten Waldes aus Buchen, Eichen und Ahorn liegt dieses Gelände mit einem Höhenunterschied von 36 Metern von einem zum anderen Ende. Das Gebäude darauf passt sich an diese Umgebung an und die Architektur wurde zu einer Abstraktion der existierenden Oberflächenform. Es sollte ein Haus entstehen, das gleichzeitig kompakt, flexibel und leicht zugänglich ist. Der Kunde detaillierte sehr genau, was er wünschte, da er nur die Hälfte der Woche hier wohnt. So wurden drei Zimmer angelegt, wovon zwei im Gebrauch und in der Größe sehr flexibel sind, zwei Bäder und eine Toilette. Das Esszimmer, das Wohnzimmer und die Küche sind Verlängerungen der Landschaft, die ins Innere dringt. Ebenso wurde eine Bibliothek, ein Büro und eine Garage für zwei Autos gewünscht. Im Inneren wurden verschiedene Materialien verwendet, Keramikfliesen, lackiertes Holz und polierter Stein.

The house is not unlike a geological element in the landscape, and rests on walls that run perpendicular to the slope.

La maison est à l'image d'un élément géologique intégré au paysage. Elle est implantée sur un terrain avec les murs perpendiculaires à la pente.

Das Haus wirkt wie ein geologisches Element in der Landschaft. Die Wände wurden senkrecht zur Neigung angebracht.

The fact that one can move the glass doors emphasizes the flexibility and dynamic nature of the house.

La possibilité de pouvoir déplacer les portes en verre exalte la flexibilité et la dynamique de la maison.

Die Glastüren können verschoben werden, was das Haus flexibler und dynamischer macht.

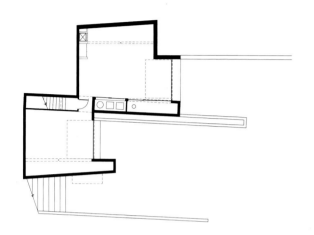

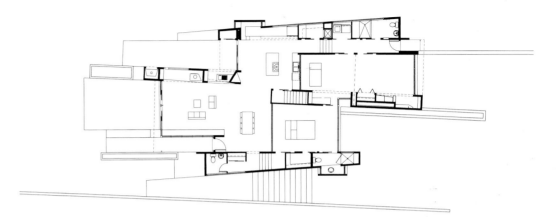

› Ground floor Rez-de-chaussée Erdgeschoss

› First floor Premier étage Erstes Obergeschoss

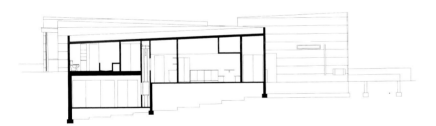

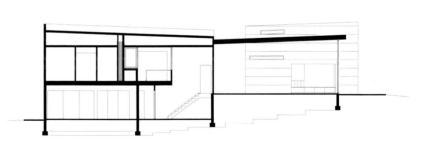

› Sections Sections Schnitte

House on Mount Fuji
Habitation sur le mont Fuji
Haus am Fuß des Berges Fuji

Narusawa, Japan

This house is located in a densely forested area at the base of Mont Fuji, and due to its volcanic past, the site is highly irregular. Architect Satoshi Okada's design is a poetic exercise in emulating nature, which led him to design a series of multiple, sinuous roofs that would mimic the irregular terrain. A large wall on a diagonal divides the house into two areas: one, a large space for common domestic functions and another zone for the bedrooms and their respective bathrooms. Upon entering the house, the visitor encounters a narrow and dark hallway which progressively widens until it is transformed into an expansive gallery illuminated from above. This space contains an attic set above the kitchen and dining room, whose ceilings, barely seven feet in hight, contrast with those in the living room, which rise sixteen feet from the floor.

Cette maison est située au pied du mont Fuji, dans une zone de végétation feuillue, peuplée d'arbres. Le terrain est accidenté dû à son passé volcanique. L'architecte Satoshi Okada a développé le projet à l'instar d'un essai poétique rivalisant avec la nature. Pour suivre cette idée, il a conçu une toiture aux multiples pentes sinueuses s'adaptant au dénivellement de terrain. Un grand mur en diagonal divise la maison en deux univers : un grand espace qui abrite les fonctions domestiques communes et une zone qui accueille les chambres à coucher et les salles de bains respectives. En entrant dans la résidence, un petit couloir s'élargit pour se transformer en une immense galerie illuminée par la lumière du soleil. Cet espace contient une soupente qui abrite la cuisine et la salle à manger, de deux mètres de hauteur à peine, contrastant ainsi avec les cinq mètres du salon.

Dieses Haus liegt am Fuße des Berges Fuji in einem Gebiet mit üppiger Vegetation und Baumbewuchs. Diese ehemalige Vulkanlandschaft ist sehr uneben. Der Architekt Satoshi Okada entwickelte die Planung wie eine poetische Übung, die die Natur nachahmt. Unter dieser Voraussetzung wurde ein Dach mit zahlreichen, kurvigen Neigungen geschaffen, das sich an die Unebenheiten des Geländes anpasst. Eine große diagonale Mauer unterteilt das Haus in zwei Bereiche: einen großen Raum, der für die gemeinsamen häuslichen Funktionen bestimmt ist und einen Bereich, in dem die Schlafzimmer und dazugehörigen Bäder liegen. Wenn man das Haus betritt, verbreitert sich der enge und dunkle Flur, um zu einer großen Galerie, in die Licht von oben fällt, zu werden. In diesem Raum gibt es eine Mansarde, in der Küche und Speisezimmer liegen. Diese beiden Räume stehen mit nur zwei Metern Höhe in einem starken Gegensatz zu dem fünf Meter hohen Wohnzimmer.

The profile of the main part of the house is clearly visible beneath the canopy of the trees and on top of the layer of lava it attempts to emulate.

Le corps de bâtiment gît clairement dessiné sous les cimes des arbres et au-dessus de la couche de lave avec laquelle il prétend rivaliser.

Der Körper liegt klar unterhalb der Baumwipfel und oberhalb der Lavaschicht, die er nachahmt.

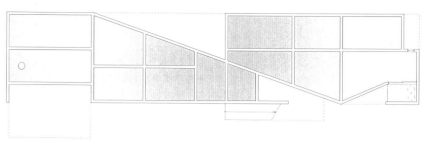

› Ground floor   Rez-de-chaussée   Erdgeschoss

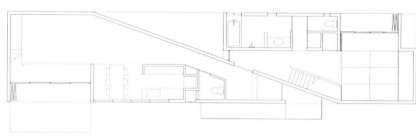

› First floor   Premier étage   Erstes Obergeschoss

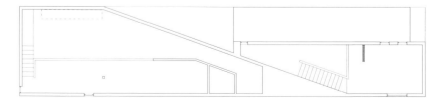

› Second floor   Deuxième étage   Zweites Obergeschoss

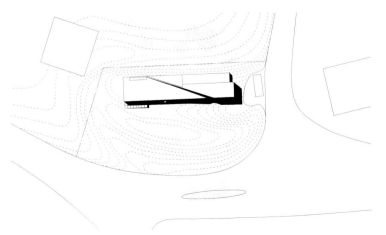

› Situation plan   Plan de situation   Umgebungsplan

The façades pull back at certain spots to create terraces, which offer views of the surroundings and a place to enjoy the outdoors.

Les façades s'effacent en certains points pour laisser la place à des terrasses qui offrent des vues sur les alentours créant ainsi une enclave pour vivre à l'extérieur.

Die Fassaden sind an einigen Punkten zurückgesetzt, um Terrassen mit Ausblick über die Umgebung zu schaffen, auf denen man sich im Freien aufhalten kann.

The light that fills the house allowed the designer to opt for finishes in dark tones, which is reflected in the furniture and decor.

La luminosité existante dans cette habitation a permis d'opter pour des finitions aux teintes sombres, à l'instar du mobilier et de quelques éléments de décor.

Da dieses Haus sehr hell ist, konnte man sich für dunkle Töne bei den Möbeln und an einigen Wänden entscheiden.

YG House
Maison YG
Haus YG

Katta-gun, Japan

This residence was conceived as a sort of three hundred-feet-long ribbon that would wrap around itself in three dimensions to create a wide open space in the middle. Six different volumes inserted into the perimeter contain all the tools necessary for domesticating this space: a kitchen, a fireplace with closets, a bathroom/laundry room, and a store room. The enclosed double-height void in the middle, without a doubt the nucleus of the house, is a thoroughly distinctive space. The rest of the rooms are only open where it is functionally necessary, while the central space communicates through vistas and via natural light with the exterior, and thus establishes unique relationships with its surroundings. The design of the house closely reflects the site: to the north, one enters the house in parallel with the topography and in contact with the earth; to the south, the house itself lifts off the ground.

Cet édifice est conçu comme une bande de ruban de quatre-vingt-dix mètres qui, en s'enroulant sur elle-même en trois dimensions, entoure un vide central. Six volumes distincts, insérés dans cette frange cernant le périmètre, contiennent les outils nécessaires pour apprivoiser l'espace : la cuisine, une cheminée armoire, un cabinet de toilette/buanderie, une salle de bains et une pièce de stockage. Le vide enfermé sur une double hauteur, noyau essentiel de la maison, est un espace insolite à l'intérieur de la maison. Les espaces de vie restants sont ouverts uniquement quand ils fonctionnent, alors que le vide central communique avec l'extérieur grâce aux vues et à la lumière naturelle, instaurant différents liens avec l'environnement. L'édifice est en relation très étroite avec le lieu sur lequel il est situé : au nord, la zone d'entrée évolue parallèlement aux courbes de niveau et est en contact étroit avec le terrain. Au sud, le volume se détache du sol.

Dieses Haus ist als eine Art neunzig Meter langes Band angelegt, das in drei Dimensionen über sich selbst gewickelt ist. Im Zentrum befindet sich ein großzügiger Leerraum. Sechs verschiedene Blöcke wurden in diesen Streifen eingebunden, in denen die notwendigen Elemente untergebracht sind, um den Raum bewohnbar zu machen, die Küche, ein Kamin-Schrank, eine Toilette-Waschraum, ein Badezimmer und eine Abstellkammer. Der Leerraum doppelter Höhe im Zentrum ist der Kern des Hauses, ein einzigartiger Raum. Die übrigen Zimmer sind nur dann offen, wenn es für ihre Funktion notwendig ist, während man von dem Leerraum im Zentrum aus einen Blick ins Freie hat und Licht einfällt. So entstehen verschiedene Beziehungen zur Umgebung. Im Norden am Eingang verläuft das Grebäude parallel zu den Kurven des Bodens und in Kontakt mit der Erde, im Süden hebt es sich vom Boden ab.

The strict geometrical lines of the house are softened by the use of wood to avoid clashing with the wooded surroundings.

La géométrie stricte des tracés de la maison est adoucie par les matériaux employés, pour la plupart des bois en harmonie avec le paysage arboré.

Die strenge Geometrie der Linien des Hauses wird durch die verwendeten Materialien gemildert. Hauptsächlich wurde Holz verwendet, das gut in die Baumlandschaft passt.

The austerity of the furnishings –due to their temporary nature– is compensated by the warmth of the wood used in the structure and interior finishes.

L'austérité du mobilier –justifiée par l'éventualité de son utilisation– est compensée par la chaleur du bois présent dans la structure et dans les finitions intérieures.

Die Schlichtheit der Möbel, die nur spärlich eingesetzt werden, wird durch die Wärme des Holzes und durch die Oberflächen ausgeglichen.

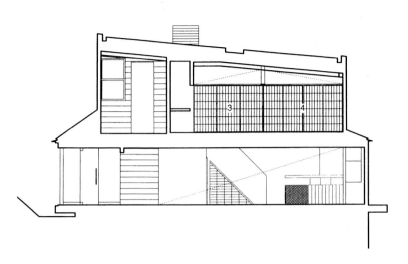 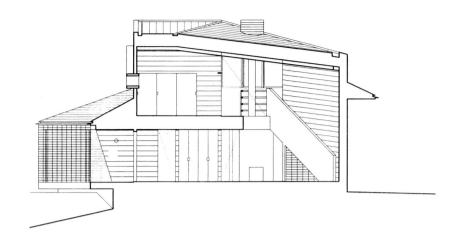

> Sections Sections Schnitte

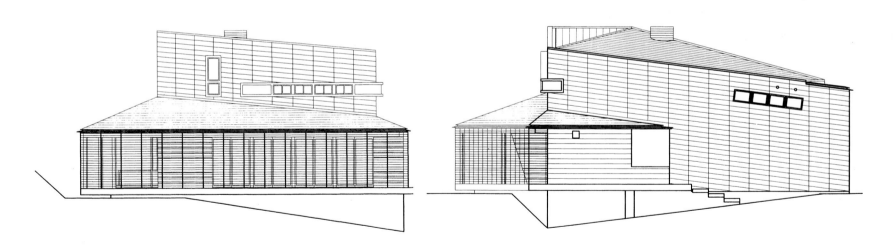

> Elevations Élévations Aufrisse

Howard House
Maison Howard
Haus Howard

Nova Sotia, Canada

The Howard House, anchored on the coastline, was built as a giant wall, inside of which the domestic functions are located. The façades of this enormous volume are covered in corrugated aluminium that was previously galvanized to protect it from rain and sea spray. The reinforced concrete foundations emerge at ground level to give shape to a skirting board that testifies to the difficulty of building in an area with such fluctuating water levels. In addition to this solid enclosure, a concrete staircase was also fixed to the main body of the house, in order to buffer the dwelling from the bitterly cold westerly winds and provide it with thermal insulation. The house's roof ascends southward, covering a continuous space that successively houses the garage, entrance courtyard, kitchen, living room and cantilevered terrace.

La maison Howard, lovée dans une enclave côtière, s'érige à l'instar d'un grand mur abritant à l'intérieur les fonctions domestiques. Les faces de cet énorme ensemble sont recouvertes d'aluminium ondulé galvanisé au préalable pour protéger le métal de la pluie et de l'air marin salé. Les fondations en béton armé émergent du terrain formant un socle révélant la difficulté d'asseoir un édifice dans une zone aux niveaux phréatiques fluctuants. A cette frange massive, s'ajoute un escalier, lui aussi en béton, adossé au corps principal qui freine les vents gelés venant de l'ouest et procure l'isolation thermique de l'habitation. La toiture, d'un seul pan, descend vers le sud couvrant un espace continu qui abrite successivement, le garage, le patio d'entrée, la cuisine, le salon et la terrasse en saillie.

Das Haus Howard liegt in Küstennähe. Es wirkt wie eine große Mauer, hinter der die verschiedenen häuslichen Bereiche untergebracht sind. Die Seiten dieses riesigen Körpers sind mit gewelltem Aluminium verkleidet, das durch Galvanisieren vor Regen und Meersalz geschützt wurde. Die Fundamente aus Stahlbeton ragen aus dem Boden heraus und bilden einen Sockel. Daran wird deutlich, wie problematisch es ist, ein Gebäude auf einem Gelände zu errichten, bei dem der Grundwasserspiegel schwankt. Außer diesem massiven Streifen wurde eine Treppe, ebenfalls aus Beton, angelegt, die sich an den Hauptkörper stützt und so die eisigen Westwinde abfängt und das Haus isoliert. Das Dach hat nur eine Neigung und steigt in Richtung Süden an. Es bedeckt den anliegenden Raum, in dem sich hintereinander die Garage, der Eingangshof, die Küche, das Wohnzimmer und die Terrasse auf einem Vorsprung befinden.

The cantilevered terrace juts out from the main reinforced concrete structure and allows the occupants to relax and take in the surrounding wilderness.

La terrasse en saillie, débordant au-dessus de la structure principale de béton armé permet de se reposer au cœur de l'environnement champêtre qui entoure l'habitation.

Die Terrasse auf dem Vorsprung, auf der man sich von der rauhen umgebenden Landschaft erholt en kann, überragt die Hauptstruktur aus Stahlbeton.

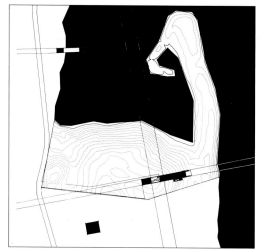

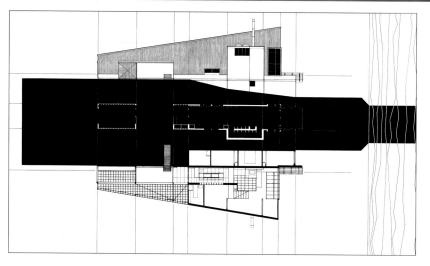

334

Into House
Maison Into
Haus Into

Espoo, Finland

This site is located on a high hill and faces west, out to sea. The outline of the house unfolds like a fan, which reflects its division into sectors. The road leads the visitor to the back part of the house, which is defined by a protective white wall. The main entrance is through a glazed incision in the main façade, reached via a metal bridge that crosses over the pool. The hallway acts as a visual and functional link between all the rooms in the house, to be seen and understood the house in its entirety, as this element connects the living areas with the more private rooms. There are a number of vertical elements related to this central piece: the stairway, crafted in steel and wood, which is a structural and sculptural masterwork; and the tower, which contains the chimneys. The latter element penetrates the entire house, and accentuates the verticality of the location, the mountain and the rugged landscape.

Ce terrain se trouve sur les hauteurs d'une colline exposée à l'ouest, vers la mer. La construction se profile, à l'instar d'un éventail déployé qui en définit clairement les secteurs. La route mène le visiteur à l'arrière de la maison, structurée par le mur blanc et protecteur. L'entrée principale est une coupure de verre dans la façade à laquelle on accède par un pont métallique qui traverse la piscine. Le vestibule est un trait d'union visuel et fonctionnel entre toutes les pièces à vivre. L'ensemble du volume est perceptible et compréhensible depuis cet espace, vu qu'il fait le lien entre le salon et les pièces plus privées. Divers éléments verticaux sont reliés à cette pièce centrale : l'escalier d'acier et de bois, œuvre empreinte de virtuosité structurelle et sculpturale et la tour qui abrite les cheminées. Cet élément traverse toute la construction accentuant la verticalité du lieu, la montagne et le paysage rocheux.

Das Grundstück liegt auf einer Richtung Westen zum Meer hin weisenden Erhebung. Das Haus ist wie ein Fächer angelegt, der klar die verschiedenen Bereiche unterteilt. Die Straße führt den Besucher zum hinteren Teil des Hauses, eine weiße und beschützende Mauer. Der Haupteingang ist ein gläserner Einschnitt in die Fassade, den man über eine Metallbrücke erreicht, die über den Swimmingpool führt. Die Eingangshalle dient als visuelle und funktionelle Verbindung für alle Räume. Von diesem Raum aus kann man das ganze Gebäude sehen und erfassen, da er die Wohnzimmer mit den privateren Räumen verbindet. Es gibt verschiedene vertikale Elemente, die mit diesem zentralen Teil in Beziehung stehen, die Treppe aus Stahl und Holz, die wie ein strukturelles und skulpturelles Meisterstück wirkt, und der Turm, in dem sich die Kamine befinden. Dieses Element durchbohrt das ganze Haus und betont die Vertikalität des Ortes, den Berg und die felsige Landschaft.

The structural organization of the house presents a network of metal columns and other vertical elements support a system of beams.

L'organisation structurelle de la maison indique un treillis de piliers métalliques et d'autres éléments verticaux qui soutient un système de poutres.

Die strukturelle Organisation des Hauses zeigt ein Flechtwerk aus Metallsäulen und anderen vertikalen Elementen, das ein Trägersystem stützt.

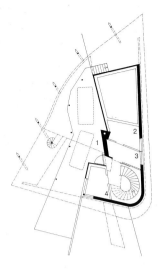

› Ground floor   Rez-de-chaussée   Erdgeschoss

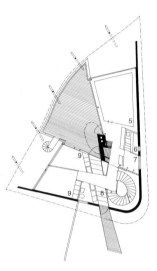

› First floor   Premier étage   Erstes Obergeschoss

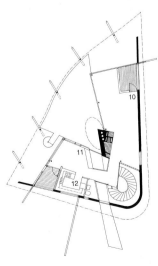

› Second floor   Deuxième étage   Zweites Obergeschoss

Rosenthal House
Maison Rosenthal
Haus Rosenthal

California, USA

The Rosenthal House-which doubles as a studio-is located right in the corner of a small triangular lot. This, in turn, led to the X-shape of the house, in order to take advantage of views towards Malibu and Palos Verdes. This recurring form allowed the designers to play with the visual combination of stairways to connect the three levels of the house: the living quarters were installed on the lower level, the first floor houses the studio, and the upper floor holds a multipurpose space. The latter, seen from the outside, resembles a lantern due to its translucent glass panels. The structure of the building-which from the exterior resembles a grotto-is framed by a concrete form that outlines the shape of the building. The stucco exterior filters daylight and creates areas of ventilation, and the light passing through the multiple openings punched in the wall casts an endless progression of fleeting images.

La maison Rosenthal, conçue comme habitation/bureau, est située juste à l'angle d'une petite parcelle triangulaire définissant la forme de l'édifice en X, avec vues sur Malibu et Palos Verdes. Cette forme récurrente instaure un jeu visuel grâce à la combinaison d'escaliers reliant les trois niveaux de la maison : le rez-de-chaussée est consacré à l'espace de vie, le premier étage accueille le studio. Le second héberge un espace polyvalent qui vu de l'extérieur ressemble à une lanterne du fait des panneaux de verre translucides qui le délimitent. La structure de l'édifice, qui, de l'extérieur, s'apparente à une grotte d'eau, est délimitée par une pièce de béton qui définit la forme de l'édifice. Le stuc extérieur permet de moduler la lumière naturelle et de créer des zones de ventilation, ainsi que de retenir des fragments d'images instantanées depuis les ouvertures créées dans le mur.

Das Haus Rosenthal ist ein Haus und Atelier auf einer Ecke eines kleinen, dreieckigen Grundstücks. Deshalb hat das Gebäude die Form eines X, und man hat einen schönen Blick auf Malibu und Palos Verdes. Die Form mit ihren Wiederholungen ermöglicht eine visuelle Kombination von Treppen, die die drei Ebenen des Hauses miteinander verbinden. Im Erdgeschoss befindet sich die Wohnung, im ersten Stock das Atelier und im zweiten Stock ein vielseitig nutzbarer Raum, der von außen aufgrund der Transparenz der Glasplatten, mit denen er verkleidet ist, das Aussehen einer Laterne hat. Die äußere Struktur des Gebäudes wirkt wie eine Wassergrotte und ist von einem Betonteil eingerahmt, das die Form des Gebäudes noch unterstreicht. Der äußere Stuck modelliert das Licht und sorgt für gute Lüftung. Gleichzeitig werden durch Öffnungen in der Wand so etwas wie Fragmente von Momentaufnahmen geschaffen.

The cross-shape of the house sets up the visual interplay of the stairways connecting the three levels of the house.

La forme en X permet de jouer visuellement avec la combinaison d'escaliers qui relient les trois niveaux de la maison.

Die X-Form ermöglicht eine visuelle Kombination von Treppen, die die drei Ebenen des Hauses miteinander verbinden.

› Ground floor   Rez-de-chaussée   Erdgeschoss

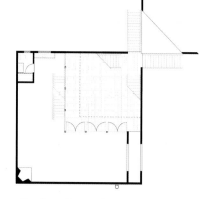

› First floor   Premier étage   Erstes Obergeschoss

› Second floor   Deuxième étage   Zweites Obergeschoss

The sensation generated by the exterior wall is the same as a set of nesting dolls, as it houses one building inside of another, as well as rooms inside of other rooms.

Le mur extérieur crée une impression similaire à celle des poupées russes, car il abrite un édifice à l'intérieur d'un autre et des espaces imbriqués les uns dans les autres.

Die äußere Mauer erinnert an eine Babuschka, denn es befindet sich ein Gebäude in dem anderen, ein Raum in dem anderen.

Y House
Maison Y
Haus Y

Yamaguchi, Japan

This house is located in a suburb that has undergone rapid growth after having evolved into a bedroom community. Its being located at the edge of a development granted the interesting possibility of opening the house to the south; the north façade juts up against the neighborhood. The house, as imagined by the architect, consists of two perpendicularly superimposed white boxes that are entirely open to the south. The ground floor is used as an entrance and social area; while the upper floor contains a bedroom, a study and the access to a large terrace spanning the roof of the lower of the two boxes. The large cantilevers caused by the recess in the glass enclosure protect the interior from direct sunlight without sacrificing its panoramic views. The openings in the walls are delicately outlined in metal and slatted shutters in the service area.

Cette habitation s'inscrit dans un quartier de la périphérie qui, sous l'effet d'un développement rapide, s'est transformé en ville dortoir. La configuration et la situation du terrain offrent des vues intéressantes permettant d'ouvrir la maison vers le sud, alors que la face nord effleure la proximité immédiate du quartier. La conception des volumes se présente sous forme de deux cubes blancs, superposés perpendiculairement et entièrement ouverts vers le sud. Le niveau inférieur sert d'accès et d'espace de réception, la partie supérieure héberge la chambre, un studio et l'accès à une vaste terrasse créée par la toiture du volume inférieur. Les grands encorbellements issus du volume enveloppé de verre permettent de protéger l'intérieur du soleil direct sans sacrifier l'étendue de la vue panoramique. Les ouvertures des murs sont délimitées par de fins profils métalliques et par des stores dans la zone des services.

Dieses Wohnhaus befindet sich in einem Außenbezirk, der sich schnell in eine Schlafstadt verwandelt hat. Da das Gebäude am Stadtrand steht, bot es sich an, den interessanten Blick nach Süden zu nutzen. Die Nordfassade zeigt jedoch direkt zum Stadtviertel hin. Es wurden zwei weiße Kästen geschaffen, die senkrecht übereinander gelegt und nach Süden offen sind. Im Erdgeschoss liegen der Eingang und die gemeinsamen Räume, im Obergeschoss die Schafzimmer, ein Atelier und der Ausgang zu einer großen Terrasse, die auf dem Dach des unteren Teils angelegt wurde. Die großen Vorsprünge, die durch das Zurücksetzen der Verglasungen entstanden sind, schützen das Innere vor direktem Sonnenlicht, ohne den wundervollen Blick zu behindern. Die Fenster an den funktionellen Räumen sind mit feinen Metallprofilen gerahmt und mit Jalousien ausgestattet.

The façade, of a great formal expressiveness, was posited as an open volume that would attempt to reflect the surrounding landscape.

La façade, dotée d'une grande expressivité formelle, se présente comme un volume ouvert qui essaie de capter le paysage extérieur.

Die Fassade mit ihrer ausdrucksvollen Form ist offen angelegt, um die umgebende Landschaft einzufangen.

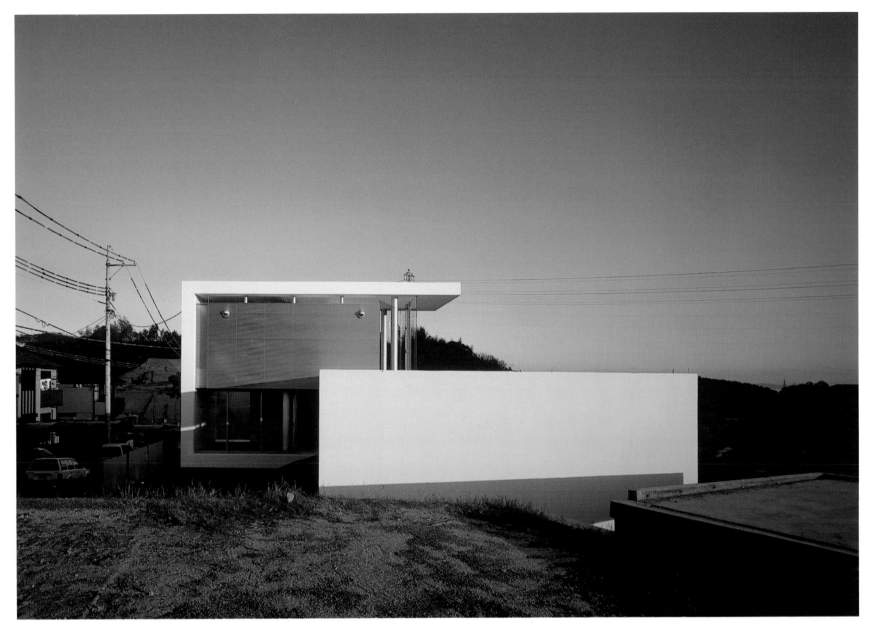

The high windows on the ground floor prevent neighboring houses from seeing in, yet also allow for air to circulate throughout the house.

Les fenêtres supérieures de l'étage inférieur masquent la vue sur les maisons voisines tout en créant une circulation d'air à l'intérieur de l'habitation.

Aus den oberen Fenstern des Erdgeschosses sieht man keine Nachbarhäuser. Sie sorgen jedoch für Luftzufuhr in der Wohnung.

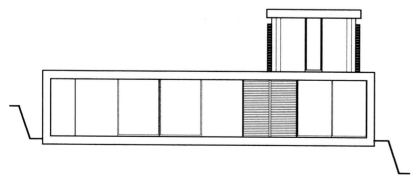

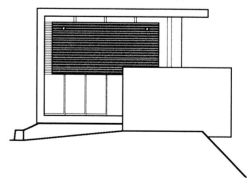

› Elevations Élévations Aufrisse

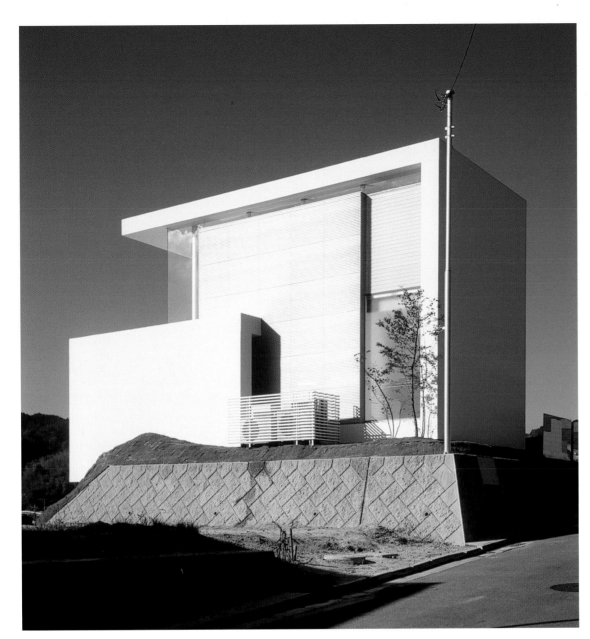

The nature of the site and the freedom it entailed were taken advantage of in full to make a succinct architectural statement.

La liberté et les conditions offertes par le terrain ont été exploitées au maximum pour concevoir un objet architectural épuré et simple.

Das Grundstück bot relativ viel Freiheit und günstige Bedingungen, um ein architektonisch sauberes und klares Haus zu bauen.

To make the most of the bright sunlight, neutral and warm colors dominate in almost all the finishes.

La dominance de tons neutres et chaleureux exalte sciemment la luminosité provenant de l'extérieur.

Die Oberflächen sind in neutralen und warmen Farben gehalten, um das vorhandene Licht noch zu unterstreichen.

An interplay of contrasts is found in this area, where warm materials, like wood, are combined with the concrete of the central wall.

Le jeu des contrastes se synthétise dans cette zone où se mêlent des matériaux chauds comme le bois et le béton du mur central.

Das Spiel mit Kontrasten wird hier noch verstärkt, indem warme Materialien wie Holz mit dem Beton der zentralen Wand kombiniert werden.

Villa Man-bow

Shizuoka, Japan

The site of this unusual house faces north, over-looking a 70° slope. The client had a clear idea of how to inhabit this space: humidity was to be kept to a minimum, the strong winds counteracted, and the chore of raking leaves in autumn avoided. To meet these ends, the architects designed two very different volumes: an elliptical sphere that would house the living areas and a rectangular parallelepiped that would be destined for use as bedrooms. Each would be raised on six columns one foot in diameter arranged in a 12 feet grid. To counteract the strong winds, the sphere, with its aerodynamic form, was designed to face the val-ley, while the rectangle was hidden amidst the trees. The copper slats that cover the sphere will take on a green patina over time, thus integrating this volume into the landscape.

Le terrain qui accueille cette habitation originale est orienté au nord et présente une pente de 70°. Le client avait une idée très précise de la concep-tion de son lieu d'habitation : contrôler au maxi-mum l'humidité, en contrecarrant la force des vents et éviter de ramasser les feuilles mortes en automne. Pour y parvenir, les architectes ont con-çu deux volumes différents sur le plan typolo-gique: une sphère elliptique pour abriter les pièces à vivre et un parallélépipède destiné aux deux chambres à coucher. Chacune d'elle s'élève au-dessus du terrain, posée sur six colonnes de 30 cm de diamètre dans un réticule de 3,6 m. Pour contrecarrer l'action des vents, le volume sphé-rique, avec sa forme aérodynamique, a été placé face à la vallée, alors que le rectangle se cache entre les arbres du bois. Les lames de cuivre, utili-sées comme revêtement extérieur de la sphère, acquérant avec le temps la patine verte inhérente à ce métal, parviennent à se fondre dans le paysage.

Das Grundstück, auf dem dieses ungewöhnli-che Haus steht, liegt Richtung Norden und hat eine Neigung von 70°. Der Kunde wusste genau, wie er diesen Ort bewohnen wollte. Die Feuchtig-keit musste so weit wie möglich unter Kontrolle gebracht werden und der Kraft der Winde musste man widerstehen, um das Laubkehren im Herbst zu vermeiden. Dazu entwarfen die Architekten zwei sehr unterschiedliche Gebäudeteile, eine elliptische Kugel für die Wohnzimmer und ein Parallelepipedon für die Schlafzimmer. Beide Teile erheben sich auf sechs Säulen mit 30 cm Durch-messer in einem Abstand von 3,6 Metern. Der kugelförmige Gebäudeteil mit seiner aerodynami-schen Form zum Tal hin lässt die Winde abgleiten, während der rechteckige Teil im Wald verborgen ist. Die Kugel ist von außen mit Kupferplatten ver-kleidet, die im Laufe der Zeit Grünspan ansetzen und sich so in die Landschaft integrieren.

The entrance to the house is a metal staircase that descends gently to the ground. The system of columns respects the existing vegetation and prevents erosion.

L'accès à l'habitation se fait par un escalier métallique posé subtilement sur le terrain. Le système de piliers respecte la couche végétale et protège le terrain de l'érosion.

Der Zugang zum Haus erfolgt über eine Metalltreppe, die leicht auf dem Gelände steht. Das Säulensystem nimmt auf die Vegetation Rücksicht und verhindert Erosion.

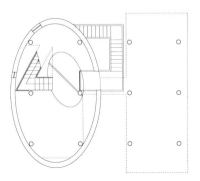
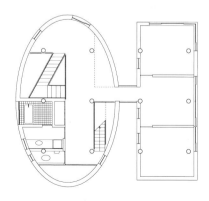
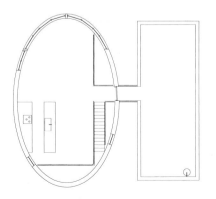

› Ground floor Rez-de-chaussée Erdgeschoss   › First floor Premier étage Erstes Obergeschoss   › Second floor Deuxième étage Zweites Obergeschoss

Inside, all the walls were finished in plaster and painted white, and then further outfitted with flexible laminated plaster veneer.

A l'intérieur, les murs sont tous plâtrés et peints en blanc et ont été revêtus de plâtre laminé.

Im Inneren sind alle Wände weiß gegipst und gestrichen und wurden mit flexiblen Gipsleisten verkleidet.

The great sensation of openness in the living room is due to its high ceilings and the absence of corners.

La sensation de largeur à l'intérieur du salon est due à la hauteur généreuse de l'espace dépourvu d'angles.

Das sehr hohe Wohnzimmer ohne Ecken wirkt sehr groß.

Tree House
Maison Arbre
Baumhaus

Cape Town, South Africa

Designing this house, located on a steeply sloping site, presented its architects with a challenge. A unique characteristic of this site, however, was its canopy of pine trees this led to the idea of designing a house in the shape of a table. Five columns designed to resemble tree trunks hold up a flat roof, from which a steel and glass skin is suspended to envelop the full volume of the house and to achieve complete transparency to the exterior. The ensemble, which rests upon a solid and enclosed stone foundation, is divided into three levels that house its various functions: in the highest part of the house, through which one enters, one finds the living room, the dining room and the kitchen. The bedrooms are on the middle level, and the ground floor, which is the area most insulated from the outside, is given over to services.

Ce projet de construction enclavée sur un terrain escarpé, a placé les architectes devant un véritable défi. La particularité de ce terrain, doté d'un baldaquin naturel formé par la cime des pins de la propriété, est à l'origine de la conception d'une maison en forme de table. Cinq piliers ont été conçus à l'instar d'un tronc d'arbre soutenant la toiture plane de laquelle pend une chrysalide d'acier et de verre qui enveloppe tout le volume dans une transparence totale vers l'extérieur. L'ensemble, qui repose sur une base massive et close en pierre, est divisé en trois niveaux accueillant les différentes fonctions : la partie supérieure, zone d'accès, héberge le salon, la salle à manger et la cuisine; la partie intermédiaire accueille les chambres et la partie inférieure, plus protégée de l'extérieur, abrite les zones de services.

Dieses Bauvorhaben auf einem schroffen Gelände stellte eine große Herausforderung für die Architekten dar. Auf dem Grundstück existiert ein natürlicher Baldachin, der von den Wipfeln der Pinien auf dem Grundstück gebildet wird. So entstand die Idee, ein Haus mit der Form eines Tisches zu entwerfen. Fünf Säulen, die den Baumstämmen gleichen, tragen ein flaches Dach, von dem eine Haut aus Stahl und Glas hängt, die das ganze Gebäude umgibt und von überall den Blick nach draußen ermöglicht. Die Gruppe steht auf einer massiven, von Stein umschlossenen Basis und unterteilt sich in drei Ebenen mit verschiedenen Funktionen. Im oberen Teil liegen der Eingang, das Wohnzimmer, das Esszimmer und die Küche, im mittleren Teil die Schlafzimmer und im Erdgeschoss die geschlosseneren Räume mit den funktionellen Bereichen.

The wooden columns branch out at the highest part of the house in an echo of the trees around them.

Les piliers de bois se ramifient en hauteur, à l'instar des arbres.

Die Holzpfeiler verzweigen sich nach oben wie die umgebenden Bäume.

Wood, which was used both in the structure and the finishes, contributes to the house's integration into the landscape.

Le bois, utilisé tant pour la structure que pour les revêtements, contribue à intégrer l'architecture au paysage.

Sowohl für die Struktur als auch die Verkleidung wurde Holz benutzt, wodurch sich das Haus gut in die Landschaft einpasst.

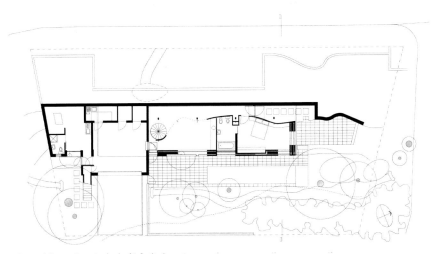

› Ground floor   Rez-de-chaussée   Erdgeschoss

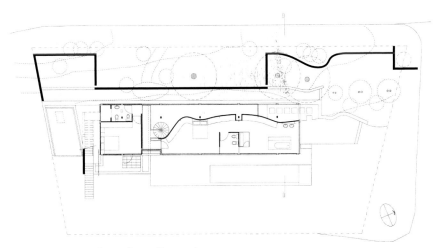

› First floor   Premier étage   Erstes Obergeschoss

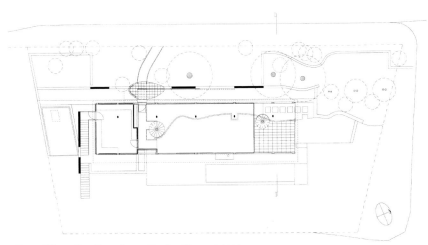

› Second floor   Deuxième étage   Zweites Obergeschoss

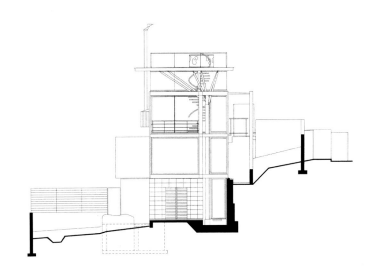

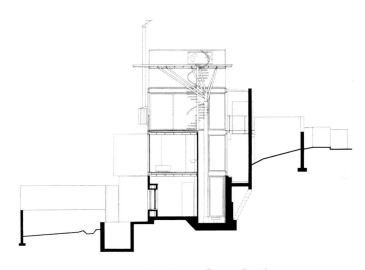

› Cross section   Section transversale   Querschnitt

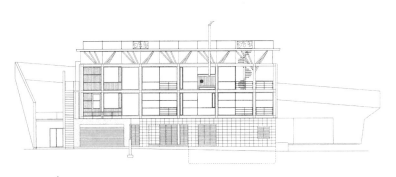

› Elevation   Élévation   Aufriss

Rose Residence
Résidence Rose
Rose Residenz

New South Wales, Australia

The Rose Residence stands on the crest of a hill, on a site that slopes symmetrically eastward and westward; it was built beside the road to take advantage of the slope of the land. The house itself is a one-storey rectangular parallelepiped that rests atop two large cement blocks serving as a skirting board-a significant part of the first floor is in cantilever as a result. The domestic programme is divided into three areas: the first zone, is reserved for the couple; the second, to the east, is for their children; and in between lie the daytime areas-the salon, dining room and kitchen. The service and storage areas, meanwhile, were cleverly fitted into the 'skirting board'. In order to have as little of an impact on its surroundings as possible, a lightweight steel structure was adopted for the house, which frames vast glass doors and windows. Displaying the beauty of the landscape from inside the house, as well as ventilating the interior and filling it with natural light.

Cette construction qui s'élève au-dessus de la crête d'une colline, sur une parcelle présentant une pente symétrique à l'est et à l'ouest, a été édifiée juste à côté de la route pour tirer parti de la pente du terrain. La typologie correspond à un parallélépipède rectangulaire d'un seul niveau appuyé sur deux grands blocs de ciment, à l'instar d'un socle, créant ainsi une large superficie en saillie. La distribution des parties domestiques s'articule en trois zones : à l'ouest, la partie destinée au couple, à l'est, celle des enfants, et la zone intermédiaire pour les espaces de jour -salon, salle à manger et cuisine-. Le socle permet d'installer les services et les espaces de rangement et de stockage. Pour réduire au minimum l'impact sur l'environnement, des structures légères d'acier encadrent les grandes portes et fenêtres de verre permettant de jouir de l'intérieur du paysage spectaculaire des alentours, de faire entrer la lumière naturelle en abondance et d'avoir une ventilation optimale.

Dieses Haus steht auf dem Gipfel eines Hügels auf einem Grundstück, das eine symmetrische Neigung von Osten nach Westen hat. Das Gebäude wurde an der Straße errichtet, um die Neigung des Geländes auszunutzen. Es handelt sich um ein Parallelepipedum mit einem einzigen Stockwerk, das sich auf zwei große Zementblöcke stützt, die den Sockel bilden. So entstand eine große Fläche auf einem Vorsprung. Der Wohnbereich ist in drei Teile unterteilt, im Westen liegen die Räume des Paares, im Osten die der Kinder und im mittleren Teil die Bereiche für den Tag, das Wohnzimmer, Esszimmer und Küche. Im erwähnten Sockel befinden sich die Installationen und Lagerräume. Um die Umgebung so wenig wie möglich zu verändern, wurde eine leichte Stahlstruktur konstruiert, die die großen Türen und Fenster umgibt. So kann man vom Inneren aus die wundervolle Landschaft genießen und gleichzeitig wird für optimales Tageslicht und Belüftung gesorgt.

A concrete platform parallels the house to offer parking, and is connected to the house by a walkway.

Il est possible de garer les voitures sur une plate-forme de béton disposée parallèlement à l'habitation à laquelle elle est reliée par une passerelle.

Auf einer Betonplattform, die parallel zum Haus verläuft und über einen Laufsteg erreicht wird, können Fahrzeuge abgestellt werden.

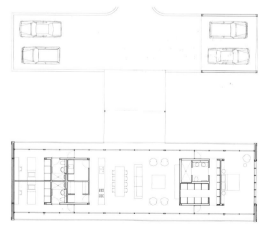

› Plan Plan Grundriss

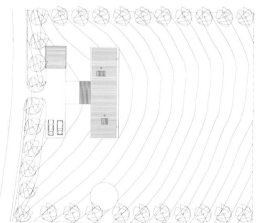

› Situation plan Plan de situation Umgebungsplan

The fact that the walls are almost entirely made of glass means that dusk turns the house into a glowing lantern on the horizon.

A la tombée de la nuit, l'immense surface de verre transforme l'habitation en un énorme foyer lumineux.

Die vielen verglasten Flächen machen aus dem Haus während der Nacht eine riesige Lichtquelle.

The south side of the house offers a striking view of Seven Mile Beach.

Du côté sud, la vue sur la plage de Seven Mile est splendide.

Von der südlichen Seite aus hat man einen überwältigenden Blick auf den Strand Seven Mile.

Photo Credits   Crédits photographiques   Fotonachweis

010-019	**Undine Pröhl**	196-201	**Ignacio Martínez**
020-027	**Barclay & Crousse**	202-209	**Matteo Piazza**
028-033	**Eric Sierins**	210-215	**Lorenzo Mussi**
034-039	**Yoshiharu Matsumura**	216-223	**José Luis Saavedra Morales**
040-047	**Hisao Suzuki**	224-231	**Christian Richters**
048-055	**Eugeni Pons**	232-241	**Edmund Sumner/View**
056-063	**Juan Purcell**	242-247	**Erich Ansel Koyama**
064-071	**Nigel Young**	248-255	**Tatsuya Noaki, Tamotsu Matsumoto**
072-077	**Hiroyuki Hirai**	256-263	**Luuk Kramer**
078-085	**Matteo Piazza**	264-273	**Ignacio Martínez**
086-093	**Katsuhisa Kida**	274-283	**Eugeni Pons**
094-101	**Alberto Piovano**	284-289	**Yoshi Shiratori/Zoom**
102-111	**John Ellis**	290-295	**Tatsuya Noaki**
112-119	**Alberto Piovano**	296-301	**Van der Merwe Miszewski Architects**
120-125	**Undine Pröhl**	302-309	**Stephen Varady, Rusell Pell**
126-133	**Geraldine Bruneel, Oussama Ayoub**	310-315	**Kevin Chu, Catherine Tighe Bogert**
134-141	**Pedro d'Orey**	316-323	**Hiroyuki Hirai**
142-149	**Joan Mundó**	324-329	**Synichi Atsumi**
150-155	**Shania Shegedyn**	330-335	**Undine Pröhl**
156-163	**Steve Keating, Eric Cobb**	336-341	**Jussi Tianen, Jyrki Tasa**
164-169	**Peter Kerze**	342-349	**Timothy Hursley**
170-175	**Undine Pröhl**	350-357	**Nobuaki Nakagawa**
176-183	**Alberto Piovano**	358-365	**Hiroyuki Hirai**
184-189	**Garofalo Architects**	366-371	**Van der Merwe Miszewski Architects**
190-195	**Matteo Piazza**	372-381	**Ross Honeysett**